DEDICATION

In ancient Greece, people with illnesses would travel to the Island of Delos and sleep in a special area devoted to Aesclepius, the Greek god of healing.

Their hope was to have Aesclepius appear to them in their dreams that night and reveal both the root causes of their illnesses as well as the cure.

To leaders everywhere . . . may The Cure serve as your modern-day trip to Delos.

THE CURE

REMEDIES FOR THE 5 AILMENTS THAT PLAGUE ORGANIZATIONS

Janet Ioli

This book is designed for informational and educational purposes only, and the material and content contained herein are sold and/or otherwise made available with the understanding that the publisher and author are not giving career, legal, or any other type of professional or personal advice of any kind. The contents of this book are derived from the author's personal experience, but neither implies nor intends any guarantee of accuracy or effectiveness. The author and publisher believe the information to be sound, but cannot be held responsible for actions taken by readers nor the results of those actions. Readers should seek competent professional advice before making any decisions. The author and publisher shall have no liability or responsibility to any person or entity with respect to any loss or damages caused, or alleged to be caused, directly or indirectly by the information in this book.

Editing, design, and layout by Matt McGovern, www.700acres.com.

Telltale Symptoms

Is Your Organization Sick?

Symptom #1: A Large Company

I am sitting in a dimly-lit banquet room with seven other executives around a round table covered by a neat, white tablecloth. We are attendees at an annual offsite meeting for top executives, and like those at the dozen or so other such tables in this expansive venue, we're all sipping either coffee or iced water.

This is the sort of meeting that occurs every year at large companies in the United States and elsewhere—the sort of meeting where senior leaders gather to outline company goals and future strategies.

I listen as several C-level executives present back-to-back on the same topics they speak about every year, using the same densely-populated PowerPoint decks crammed with talking points prepared by others. Some add a dose of humor or inflection, which helps keep the drowsiness away, while others simply drone on.

Invariably, when we get to the Q&A portion of each presentation, instead of audience members raising the real issues on their minds, only polite, politically-correct fodder or posturing takes place—and that's if there are any murmurings at all. I can only surmise that most of my colleagues fear they might say something controversial or, worse yet, cause others to question their commitment and loyalty. Besides, the meeting is already running long. As usual, the company is trying to cover far too much in just a day-and-a-half.

A dull energy permeates the room. People nod and smile as if programmed. With too few breaks and too little interaction, the attention span of most audience members wanes.

When finally there is a break, the refreshment table becomes an oasis that's approached with fervor. Most know they need a liberal dose of sugar and coffee to get through the next three-and-a-half hours.

Does this scenario sound familiar?

As a facilitator, coach, observer, or actual participant, I have attended countless such meetings—so much so that I'd wager even if I didn't know which organization's meeting I was attending, I could predict the order of each presentation, the content, and the kinds of questions (or lack thereof) likely to be raised.

Sadly, year after year, from one large company to another, this dynamic is repeated far too often.

With a captive audience, efforts by presenters to incite connection, inspiration, and excitement rarely factor in—engaging the human element becomes irrelevant. As for audience members, they feel bound to the company by "golden handcuffs," fortunate to have the paychecks, large bonuses, and perks that come with their executive titles. Words that connect to their wallets spark the most interest, while words that inspire and evoke emotions do not.

Symptom #2: A Religious Institution

I am sitting in a pew at church, observing a typical Sunday mass. The priest reads his sermon and guides attendees in ritual. In turn, the audience members recite their portions dutifully, standing and sitting on queue.

The priest's unwavering, monotone delivery has most attendees in trance-like states. Their eyes appear glazed and my hunch is most are not engaged or really hearing what the priest is saying.

The sermon continues—a message about duty and compliance, with fear-based consequences for non-compliance. People mumble words and whisper songs as directed, as if programmed for many years, and still the priest's tone remains unchanged.

The lack of engagement by both the priest and churchgoers is pronounced. I can almost feel the energy draining from the room, leaving the air dull and stale. Yet duty and compliance prevail—only once the service is over do people begin to slip out. Their weekly obligation fulfilled, now it's time to get back to their real lives.

Over the years, I have attended services for many religious organizations, finding this pattern of ritual and compliance commonplace.

Because the audience is captivated by tradition and fear, inspiration and connection is rarely a factor. Attendees are bound by dutiful obedience already, and fear the consequences of any perceived misalignment.

Symptom #3: A Large University

I am sitting in an auditorium-style classroom at a large university. This is a required class for the degree program, so the room is packed with students.

The professor stands behind a podium and drones on about various reading assignments and research. He seems oblivious to the tone and energy of the young bodies and minds with him in the room.

Some students dutifully take notes in hopes of capturing the professor's words so they can be regurgitated to him on exams. Others pull out electronic devices and glance at them covertly, trying not to get caught. Still others whisper to their neighbors or gaze off into space.

The students are captive—they need to be here, after all—so any attention the professor might give to the human element and dynamic in the room is irrelevant. Inspiring the students doesn't seem all that necessary to him. Instead, he believes their desire for a degree should be sufficient to hold their interest.

Eyes begin to wander to the clock at the front of the room, as though the timepiece is the Times Square Ball and the New Year's Eve countdown is underway.

10 – 9 – 8 – 7 . . .

When the bell rings at last, the sounds of bustling chatter and shuffling feet mark the end of class. Mercifully, only five more sessions remain, plus the final exam to get credit, and then each student can check this course off his or her required list.

Does this sound like your experience in college, or perhaps a situation your child currently faces?

Sadly, this pattern is commonplace in many colleges and universities.

What Do These Symptoms Tell Us?

Take a closer look at each of these meetings. Can you see the symptoms of underlying, deadly ailments—the kind of ailments that infect even the most well-meaning and adept leaders, spreading like epidemics and becoming commonplace?

These ailments drain energy, kill enthusiasm, and cause robot-like behavior, along with a host of other organizational ills. As a result, employee and constituent engagement mirrors these disease states and stays low despite extensive and oft-expensive initiatives and good-faith efforts to control engagement like a commodity.

If you lead an organization, or are simply part of an organization, you are familiar with these symptoms and with the subsequent ailments I'm about to describe. You experience them and live them every day. In fact, they may have become so much a part of the fabric of your organization that they seem "normal" to you.

And yet the bold truth is that your organization—most organizations—are sick.

Yes, sick.

Isn't it time for a cure?

Let's take a closer look . . .

Real-World Scenario: Do You Know "Roger?"

Roger is the president of an information technology company division that boasts 30,000 employees and $5 billion a year in revenue. He has worked his way up the ranks in this company and is known as a "brilliant mind," strategic thinker, and someone who can "make things happen."

He faces extraordinary revenue growth challenges, much pressure to demonstrate sustained business performance, a shrinking budget, and fewer and fewer resources to make all of this happen.

His external competitors are increasing, his existing customers are facing budget issues of their own, and differentiation in the marketplace is becoming increasingly more difficult.

Talented employees are hard to find, especially ones who are committed, innovative, and prudent risk-takers—the kind of employees who care enough about a company and its future not to just go through the everyday motions of punching a clock to get a paycheck.

Culture Check

Roger has initiatives in place designed to create a workplace where people feel valued and connected. All the things a good leader should focus on—Engagement, Diversity, Ethics, Flexible Workplace, Wellness, Mentoring, and Employee Development are being addressed. Yet the results from metrics in place to measure these intangibles don't reflect the enormous effort being made and dollars being spent. Indicators point to "company leaders" being deficient in good people leadership.

"So," Roger figures, "if we do more leadership training and develop our leaders, this engagement connection will result."

Another initiative to strengthen the company's leadership ensues— replicating with a slightly different flavor the same initiatives to improve leadership that were instituted by the previous Roger and the "Rogers" or "Rachels" before him.

Yet despite what organizational history is telling him, Roger is convinced his approach is different and will somehow save the day. Remember, if anyone can make things happen, it is Roger . . . or so he has been told.

Tone

Middle managers and lower level executives secretly balk at yet another attempt to "fix the leaders." They have been sent to training, been to leadership off-sites, and been surveyed and "360-feedbacked" to death.

They are skeptical and tired of all the initiatives, but resign themselves to silently shake their heads, follow orders, and simple "play the game"—too worried about losing their jobs and having to retool their own resumes and match their salaries in such an unsteady job market. They feel overworked and underappreciated, and are fatigued by all the bureaucracy and the constant changes in direction. They dare not say what they really think, and nod in agreement at meetings even when they don't quite understand why they're meeting.

They don't feel involved or heard, so why rock the boat? After all, it's not their boat anyway, they rationalize . . .

The general employee population is burnt out and tired, too. They sense an inauthentic, political tone in the air and don't really trust their organization's leaders to look out for their best interests and care about them as human beings.

They want to consider their jobs as more than just paychecks. They want to view their jobs as learning and development opportunities, and don't want to stay in one position too long or be viewed as a "resource."

They want to be rewarded and recognized for their efforts. They want to be challenged. Their leaders seem tired, overly busy, reactive, burnt out, and unable to coach them to steer their careers. They don't understand why the organization is so fixated on engagement surveys and department "action plans." They just want a work environment in which they can contribute fully, feel connected and included, and know that someone cares about their growth and advancement.

It's Time to Get Real

More often than not, good or better leadership is the remedy prescribed for organizational ailments that have to do with people. The presumption is that good leaders can provide appropriate cures for chronic "people problems," resulting in greater productivity and increased employee engagement.

Companies either promote and assign their own internal leaders or hire them from the outside. Government agencies look to their elected or appointed leaders. Churches and religious organizations look to their clergy or spiritual leaders. Universities look to their Deans.

There are a gazillion books on leadership out there, and probably too many seminars, workshops, and classes on how to be a better leader. The main themes all run together, and most leaders have read at least one of the most popular books and have attended numerous workshops.

The fact is, if you're a leader in an organization today, you probably already know some or much of the theories or varying musings on what it takes to be a good leader—or you can at least find a great book that lays out the requisite skills.

You don't need yet another book to tell you what the skills and behaviors are.

Applying them, however, is a different story.

Here is a simple question for you, and the core premise of this book:

Do you see the silent engagement epidemic raging in your organization and how your leadership behavior can cure it?

Why You Should Read this Book

While there are many great books about leadership available, the last thing we need is another one. So, you may be thinking, "Why did you write this book and why should I read it?"

In my work as an executive coach, leadership and organizational development professional, and a human resources executive in and with organizations in numerous industries over the past 20-plus years, I have observed the same people-related "ailments" and themes over and over. Every organization thinks their ailments are unique to them and that others just "don't understand" the uniqueness of the issues they face. So they keep trying to rationalize and blame "external" conditions as the cause.

Funny thing is, though, the same exact ailments have been around since I came onto the scene, and they were around for many years before that. The only difference is that they have become more severe and more pronounced because the environments in which we operate are more complex and because we fail to apply consistent remedies over time.

So why isn't the prescription of better leadership taking hold?

- I have worked with thousands of leaders on the inside of different organizations in various industries.

- I have coached leaders who faced the same issues and circumstances, all adamant about how unique their situations were.

- I have conducted myriad leadership workshops and asked leaders to identify their top leadership challenges and the problems that plague them.

- I have worked with executive teams transitioning into new leadership roles.

- I have observed, participated in, or facilitated countless executive team strategy and planning processes and retreats.

Regardless of the industry or type of business, the same themes or "ailments" always emerge.

So what gives?

In this practical and non-theoretical book, I share with you and describe the five common leadership ailments that plague many of today's large organizations, present their symptoms, pinpoint their main causes, and provide a treatment plan for each.

This book is not about how to manage your business or execute a plan effectively. It's not a book about how to manage or how to lead.

This book is about the effect on organizations when leaders don't role model, practice, and embody basic leadership behaviors.

It is about the impact you have as a leader, and it's an invitation to learn, apply, and embody leadership behaviors to cure the epidemic raging silently under the surface of your own organization.

This book is low on theory and long on real, practical observations and solutions. You will certainly recognize the ailments as I identify and describe them. Perhaps you will be amused by my candor since leaders rarely talk about these kinds of things openly, relegating them instead to their growing lists of organizational initiatives designed to address this or that challenge.

As a leader, there's simply not enough time in the day, week, month, or year to stick with the status quo. As a leader, it's time to get real.

- Call the ailments in organizations what they are and talk about what leadership behaviors contribute to their appearance.

- Talk about leadership remedies.

- Talk about leadership as a cure for the five ailments plaguing our organizations.

- Talk about what you can do now, right away, to stop the epidemic.

Most of all, let's talk about *you* as . . . *The CURE.*

This book outlines five common organizational ailments.

It describes each ailment, identifies its common symptoms and main cause, and provides a leadership remedy and treatment plan for each.

Organizational Ailment	Leadership Cause(s)	Leadership Remedy & Treatment Plan
#1 Robot Syndrome *(Page 21)*	Loss of Real Human Connection	Connection: Stay Plugged In • Presence • Purpose • Proficiency • People
#2 "In No One We Trust" Toxicity *(Page 77)*	Absence of Authenticity	Authenticity: Open Your Kimono • Transparency • Tact • Touch
#3 Yes-itis *(Page 115)*	Failure to Empower Others	Empowerment: Loosen the Reins • Risk • Result • Reward
#4 Blame Disorder *(Page 151)*	Fear of Failure	Accountability: Expect & Own Mistakes • Acknowledgement • Awareness • Advancement
#5 Energy Breakdown *(Page 187)*	Burnout	Balance: Honor Your Energy • Listen • Limit • Laugh

Directions & Potential Side Effects

Please Read Carefully

During these treatments, you will undergo deep introspection and self-evaluation as you prepare to be cleansed of the enlarged ego toxins resulting from the five ailments.

Side effects may be extreme discomfort, denial, judgment about the stupidity of this entire exercise, and belligerent criticism of this book.

You may experience thoughts of depression or illusions of grandeur, believing that you already know all the answers to some of the questions and that this is elementary since you have been a leader for many years and are beyond all of this.

None of these side effects are serious or fatal, so please ignore them and persist. You will find that the small but potent ego toxins may be deeply ingrained and hard to shake at first.

Perseverance and adherence to the treatment plans within each remedy will get you through the initial shock to your system, the ego toxins will begin to dissipate, and side effects will subside over time.

It is critical that you do not skip any treatment or skim over them, as these ailments are very resistant to treatment and can easily re-emerge if not addressed thoroughly.

Ailment #1: Robot Syndrome

Will the Real Humans Please Stand?

We have been learning socio-cultural norms all our lives. We learn which behaviors are acceptable and which aren't in certain social situations or cultures. Even our organizations have their own social and cultural norms, which are usually established by the tone the leader sets.

In large, bureaucratic organizations, something mysterious happens as leaders move up the management hierarchy. As they hit the executive level, an invisible aura of royalty suddenly emerges, and the leader is no longer treated like a regular human being. He or she becomes an instrument of the organization, surrounded by robotic minions who create rituals and "processes" designed to make life easier for the leader and to shield him or her from day-to-day realities.

As time becomes more precious for the executive, the leader begins to rely on these underlings more and more. They write the leader's speeches, create his or her presentations, and screen all interactions. Reality becomes filtered and colored by their spin.

The robotic minions welcome the role they play. They feel empowered by the leader's royal aura. Interactions with commoners and the leader are carefully shielded and scripted. They don't want to risk public embarrassment for the leader or, even worse, have the leader say something that's not scripted and reviewed by them in advance.

Meetings take on a mechanical quality. Their main goal is to follow the robotic minion's prescribed protocol and not upset the established order. To question or have conversations outside this prescribed protocol is considered a challenge verging on insubordination.

Initiatives are established for everything that needs human attention. If the organization lacks diversity of thought or composition, a diversity initiative is established. If ethics breaches are in the news, an ethics initiative is rolled out. If a major quality issue costs the company money, then a quality initiative is put in place to prevent a recurrence.

Through these well-intentioned, stove-piped, disconnected "initiatives," the robotic minions are able to establish order and a process for the leader to address various organizational ills that crop up.

Now, it's not that the robotic minions have evil intentions. Quite the contrary, their reason for being is to protect the leader and make sure things run smoothly.

The leader welcomes these robotic minions and their loyal and devoted assistance. Theirs is a co-dependency that perpetuates and unintentionally turns organizations into dysfunctional robotic states.

> *To be successful, organizations know they need their people to feel connected, but no engagement initiative can work when an organization suffers from Robot Syndrome.*

Over time, the leader's true voice gets lost, and the only voice employees actually hear is an airbrushed, scripted version—a twelfth-hand interpretation of what the leader actually means to communicate. Much like the Wizard of Oz, people only see an illusion and not the real thing.

Operating in this robotic state for long has consequences:

- Real human connections falter.

- Initiatives become nothing more than meaningless, bureaucratic exercises.

- Conversations turn superficial and stay on the surface.

- Presentations follow similar formats and rarely deviate in tone or language.

- Employees imitate the approved language and begin to use words they don't really understand.

- Dialog becomes programmed and statements are couched with platitudes.

- Fear of being ostracized or not fitting in runs rampant.

- The magic cord connecting us as humans—that "plugs" us into a collective energy—gets unplugged.

I call this cord the "engagement cord." It plugs into our hearts and souls and triggers feelings of caring and commitment. This is the cord organizations seek when they spend many millions of dollars on initiatives to make people feel more engaged and committed. To be successful, they know they need their people to feel connected.

Sadly, no engagement initiative can work when an organization suffers from Robot Syndrome.

Here's what is critical to understand about this ailment:

For some reason, when we work and lead in organizations, we choose to ignore certain fundamentals about how human beings operate and behave. We pretend these fundamentals either don't exist or don't matter, that they are "fluffy" or have no place in business or academia or government or in other institutions. *"We* are here to produce results," we maintain. *"We* are here to lead."

While I agree that businesses exist to produce results, the fundamental fallacy in that thinking is obvious: *Who* is here to produce results? *Who* is here to lead the organization?

People are . . . and unless organizations take the time to understand and address important underlying human dynamics, organizational results will be compromised forever. Robot Syndrome can only be treated by accepting the premise that we are by nature not robots, and therefore cannot be treated like them.

What is Robot Syndrome?

Robot Syndrome is a condition that manifests in organizations that neglect the human element and lose human connection.

When a leader ignores or minimizes the people aspects and dynamics associated with key decisions or activities, the cord of human connection necessary for sustained success and engagement becomes "unplugged."

Common Symptoms

- Use of words that no one understands or that de-humanizes their meanings

- Admonishment of human needs

- Compartmentalization of "work" and "real" personas as two distinctly different identities and acknowledgement of only the "work" persona

- Indifference to mood, inspiration, or real tone/energy of a group

- Maximization of bottom-line results, metrics, and business-only language in interactions with a minimization of need for human connection and inspiration

- Conflict avoidance

- Subordination of the "human element" and the understanding of basic human behavior

Contributing Factors

The following conditions contribute to the development of leadership behaviors that lead to chronic Robot Syndrome:

- Personal insecurity

- Leader isolation

- Status consciousness

- Over-reliance on protocol

- Singularly-focused emphasis on results

- Viewing people as expendable resources

- Bias for efficiency

- Limits on time

- Fear

> ## *Main Cause of Robot Syndrome:*
> Loss of Real Human Connection

ROBOT SYNDROME
Leadership Remedy & Treatment Plan

If your organization is afflicted with Robot Syndrome, then you as the leader are the main carrier. You must rid yourself of this ailment before you can begin to heal the organization and eventually wipe it out. Doing so will take much effort, diligence, and soul searching, but the impact will be far-reaching and critical to the overall health and sustainability of your organization.

Ailment #1: Robot Syndrome

Leadership Remedy:
Connection—Stay Plugged In

Treatment Plan:

* Presence
* Purpose
* Proficiency
* People

Prognosis:
Advice Following Treatment

Robot Syndrome Leadership Remedy: Connection—Stay Plugged In

The *Leadership Remedy* for Robot Syndrome is Connection.

The *Treatment Plan* consists of examining the four "P"s: Presence, Purpose, Proficiency, and People.

Presence

- How deeply comfortable are you in your own skin in all types of circumstances?

- Do you stay centered, composed, and focused when things are off kilter?

- What type of energy are you carrying and transmitting to others?

- What sort of container do you carry yourself around in and what societal message does it send?

Purpose

- Are you clear about what your unique contribution is?

- Do you fully bring that contribution to the table?

Proficiency

- Do you have depth of knowledge and mastery of a particular area or domain?

- Do you continuously seek to learn, grow, and expand your expertise and capacity?

People

- Do you genuinely care about and connect with other people?

- Do you find value in others and their contributions and deeply listen to, honor, and learn from their perspectives even when they are different from your own?

- Do you feel and show empathy and compassion for others?

Ailment #1: Robot Syndrome

Leadership Remedy: Connection—Stay Plugged In

Treatment Plan:

- Presence
- Purpose
- Proficiency
- People

Prognosis: Advice Following Treatment

"We convince by our presence." (Walt Whitman)

Robot Syndrome Treatment Plan: *Presence*

Summary

This part of the Robot Syndrome treatment plan is designed to help you understand "presence" and examine how the energy of your presence manifests in your self, your outward appearance and physical container, and your interactions with others. The more attuned to you are to your pure energetic self, the more able you are to release insecurities and genuinely connect with others.

Goal

To bring forth the real, centered part of "you" and to be open, present, and human.

Real-World Scenario: Do You Know "Dan?"

Dan looked as though he was an executive. He sported designer suits and had an impeccable appearance that exuded affluence and status. His demeanor commanded attention and respect, and his smile and charm topped off the overall polished impression. His presentation skills were smooth and his command of language convinced others of his credibility and competence.

Once you spent time with Dan, though, the first impression didn't fit the experience. The more you interacted with him, the more you realized he lacked true substance, depth, and empathy. You began to realize the real Dan was very different from his public persona. Despite the polished façade, he lacked true presence.

Most of us have a "Dan" (or two) in our lives.

The Ego

As humans, each of us learns to interact and view our surroundings from some frame of reference, or lens. We also learn how to survive, both physically and emotionally, and to adapt or influence our circumstances in order to ensure that survival. We do this by developing what is often referred to as "ego strength."

The word ego often conjures negative connotations or associations. When we hear it, we usually think "self-centered," "arrogant," or someone who is "full" of him- or herself. In reality, though, ego is the Greek word for "I," which means "one's identity and self" and "a thinking, feeling, conscious being, able to distinguish itself." *(Source: Dictionary.com)*

Your own concept of your identity—or your ego—has a lot to do with you and your leadership. Ego is your sense "self." It makes you who you are and is shaped by a host of different things.

There are varying theories about its formation, but theorists tend to agree that we develop a sense of self over time, and the interactions we have with our childhood caregivers influence our ego's strength dramatically.

For example, responses to stress and emotions in childhood form neural wiring patterns and get stored as unconscious responses and associations that influence our behaviors as we grow. In fact, many of the behaviors we exhibit today likely result from this early learning, and we may not even realize these embedded responses exist!

The good news is that our neural patterns can be rewired.

As we grow to adulthood, the hope is that our sense of self strengthens and develops, and we learn to respond to stress productively and integrate and adapt to change. Ego strength is critical, as it allows us to feel confident and comfortable enough with ourselves to allow us to act in non-defensive ways.

Therein lies the paradox.

The greater sense of self or ego-strength you have, the more you can deal with the ebbs and flows of life. The less developed your sense of self, the more likely you are to be characterized incorrectly as having a "big ego" when, in fact, just the opposite is true. Our reactive, protective, controlling, and defensive behaviors come from places of fear and survival, and from lack of sufficient ego strength to offer us choice. They are actually the result of a less developed and more primitive sense of self (or ego).

Ego and Presence

Most leaders move into leadership roles in organizations as a reward for doing something really well, or for serving an organization for a long time, or they are technically competent in a particular area and have been doing it longer than everyone else, or are simply good at making things happen in a bureaucratic environment. They usually put in the effort and time that others can't, don't, or won't, and are seen as reliable and dependable. They may have good internal networks and are often known and visible to the decision-makers picking the people being put into leadership positions. In some cases, leaders become leaders because they happen to be in "the right place at the right time" or know the "right person" when a decision is being made.

Whether or not someone possesses core leadership traits and abilities is often an afterthought when selecting a leader. Rather, the focus is usually on developing leadership skills *after* a person has been selected.

We rarely factor in having a strong sense of security with self and with one's abilities, when presence is actually one of the qualities most needed by leaders so they can focus on the development and performance of others, which is critical to organizational success.

Leaders also require emotional maturity, emotional intelligence, confidence, the ability to collaborate, and personal resilience, but without a deeply developed sense of self, without presence, a leader's security may be fragile, and under stress and pressure he or she may exhibit reactive insecurity. This could manifest itself as over self-protection, conflict avoidance, a need to over-please, and a tendency to over-control people and situations. Leaders who lack presence also tend to inflate their personal capabilities. They come off as narcissistic, arrogant, or "full of themselves."

Your Demeanor

How you carry yourself is an important part of how others perceive your presence.

You can fake outer confidence and exude false bravado and an attitude that makes others think you're invincible. You can walk around with an intimidating posture and hold your head as though you're looking down on others. Like our friend "Dan," you can dress spectacularly and wow people with how put together you are. You can even name drop and spout impressive lists of places you have been, trendy things you do, and things you claim to know.

You can appear as the epitome of perfection on the outside—the way you think others think an executive should act and dress—and others may perceive you as having a strong presence, but inside you may be insecure, ungrounded, and unsure. You may seek constant validation and be trying to prove your worth continuously by showing/telling others how worthy you are. You may feel threatened by the slightest challenge to your image and standing . . . and the Robot Syndrome actually helps you maintain the act.

As a leadership treatment, you must get in touch with your deep, authentic presence—the type of presence that comes from the inside, and that all the prepping and primping and glossing on the outside, while important, can't give. You may appear to have it, but only deep work on your self will develop your true and authentic presence.

Without such internal grounding, you will be a shallow, albeit convincing, shell, and your tendency to exhibit the Robot Syndrome—the perfect vehicle for disguising your deep insecurity with yourself—will be magnified.

What Is Real Presence?

Your real presence consists of three important elements:

- Your Connection to Your Self

- Your Physical Container

- Your Connection to Others

Your Connection to Your Self

Connection to your self is perhaps the most critical of the three presence attributes, as it is the most foundational.

Being present means. . .

- Being and staying fully "plugged in" to who you really are at the deepest, purest level and bringing that part of yourself forward in every aspect of your life.

- Transcending all of your petty needs, wants, attachments, to-do lists, and power plays to bring your full self—body, heart, mind, and spirit—into the present moment and directing all of your energy and full attention to what you are doing or who you are with.

- Coming from that place within where your racing thoughts, fears, anxieties, insecurities, personal agendas, and judgments are set aside.

- Connecting to a universal energy and being deeply grounded in the certainty of what you are doing so that you can harness and direct all aspects of your being at any given moment.

If this sounds too ethereal, too "out there," or impractical, trust me, it's not. Quite the contrary.

I'm sure you've heard athletes and performers talk about being "fully present" or "in the flow" when they recount their greatest accomplishments. Such a state comes from bringing your full awareness, energy, confidence, competence, and purest self to the present moment; from putting aside all doubts, insecurities, fears, judgments, and attachments to pre-planned outcomes.

In that moment you are fully open, concentrating, and focused on what you are doing and the experience of doing it. You are not worried about what others think, how you look, or about playing a part. You are completely, purely present with positive intent and no judgments.

When you are able to capture the moment and bring forward the purest form of your self, you have connected to your self.

Treatment Application:
10 Tips to Connect to Your True, Energetic Presence

1. **Quiet Your Mind.** Your mind never stops. It is hard to connect to your true nature when your mind is racing and filled with judgments, anxiety, and tasks. Sit back, take a deep breath, close your eyes, and visualize something beautiful in nature. See a sunset in your mind's eye, or imagine you are walking on the beach near the ocean. Picture a forest with the leaves changing colors in all of fall's magnificence. There is nothing like the beauty and awe of nature to bring us back to our personal center of gravity.

2. **Clarify What You Stand For.** Everything we do and say is part of who we are and how others see us, and manifests as our presence. Are your daily actions and words congruent with who you want to be and what you stand for? Make a list of what is important to you, what you want to be known for, and the attributes you want others to use to describe you.

3. **Look in the Mirror.** Take a regular inventory of your behavior, words, and actions. Are you living up to what you say and want to stand for? If not, why not? What do you need to *start doing?* What do you need to *stop doing?*

4. **Forgive and Validate Yourself.** You can't connect when you are too busy doubting yourself or beating yourself up. If you are not kind to and appreciative of yourself, how can you expect others to be? Similarly, how can you be that way with others?

5. **Let Go of Fear.** Fear is the number one killer of true energetic presence. It destroys self-confidence, initiative, innovation, and

purity of action. It paralyzes us and keeps us caged. Replace fear with courage to act, courage to make mistakes, courage to stand in confidence. Expect failure and mistakes as part of the experience of success.

6. **Set Clear Intentions.** We often go through our days without thinking, without taking the time to ponder and decide what it is we want to manifest. We act without considering the consequences of our actions in advance. Make a commitment to be more deliberate about your actions and the behaviors you want to emulate. Describe what kind of person you want to be and list the actual behaviors you want to exhibit.

7. **Bring Your Full Attention to Everything.** Are you proud of your ability to multi-task? Don't be. Practice focusing on one thing at a time for a week. Notice your mind wandering and bring it back. Put away the smart phone and pay attention to the details you never see. Experience what is happening right now, as though this is the last moment you will ever have.

8. **Stay Centered.** Fear, anxiety, self-doubt, insecurity, and the dramas associated with living cause us to get off-kilter and disconnect from our true selves. Practice coming back to that place inside that cannot be swayed or uprooted by all these things swirling in your mind. Close your eyes and imagine your feet are glued to the ground with deep roots planted beneath them. Take a deep breath and feel how solid and steady you are. Picture a giant redwood tree—majestic and firmly planted. Now come to that place inside—majestic and firmly planted.

9. **Listen Deeply.** Listening deeply requires not only hearing, but also your full attention, focus, and energy. Listening requires you to quiet your mind and put away your racing thoughts and

self-consciousness so you can be totally present when someone is talking to you.

10. **Stop Comparing.** The comparing game starts when we are toddlers. We measure our worthiness, talents, beauty, and everything else by comparing ours to theirs. If we deem someone better, then we must be NGE (not good enough).

    The more you compare, the more you shrink and disconnect from the light that is your true essence. Focus on what you bring, what makes you unique, and stop holding a measuring stick up to others as your self-sabotaging weapon.

Your Physical Container

Everyone has a physical "container" in which his or her energetic presence is embodied. This is where the outward appearance of presence comes in, and the area on which we tend to focus the most.

How you look, what you wear, the condition of your body, how you carry yourself, your body language, your mannerisms, your vocal quality and tone, and many other attributes make up the outward container of your presence.

Make no mistake, whether we like it or not, outward appearance is important and should not be dismissed as insignificant.

Outward appearance sends socio-cultural and socio-economic messages to others and may be the only piece of our presence we expose to others initially. Some of these messages are intended, some unintended.

Luckily, we can control many of the factors that influence our physical containers, helping to ensure the messages we send align with the internal components of presence.

The key here is not to focus solely on this aspect of presence. Outward appearance is the *container*, not the essence, of presence.

Treatment Application:
Top 10 Physical Presence Self-Assessment

1. Does my outside appearance reflect who I am on the inside?

2. Do I take care of and honor my body as the important vessel that holds me inside it?

3. Do I consider my health to be of upmost importance and attention, and recognize it as the foundation that enables my existence and contribution?

4. What socio-cultural messages does my grooming and appearance send to others?

5. Are the messages sent by my physical container consistent with the impact I want to have on the world?

6. Is my appearance hindering my impact on the world? If so, in what ways?

7. What actions do I need to take to align my energetic essence with my outward container?

8. What changes do I need to make to align my grooming and appearance with socio-cultural expectations of the leadership role I am in?

9. How do I express my individuality and uniqueness with my outward container while acknowledging and accommodating socio-cultural norms?

10. What immediate steps do I need to take to make my health and physical body of paramount importance?

Your Connection to Others

We have learned that your energy and how you direct it is a part of presence relating to how you connect to yourself. We've also learned that your container is what you carry your energy in. Now we take a look at what you say and the quality of how you relate to others, or your ability to "plug in" and connect to the deepest essence of other people.

Of course, unless you can first plug in and connect to your own self, you cannot tap into and connect to others at the deepest levels.

Do you listen to others, or do you always do the talking? Are you curious about their lives, their stories, their interests, what makes them tick? Do you tend to judge or criticize? Do you seek to control every situation, or do you appreciate and acknowledge the contribution of others and what's happening around you?

If every moment, every interaction, is all about you; if you don't engage others and treat them as full partners in your life, you cannot connect to their essence . . . and if you fail to connect with others, you cannot be fully present.

Treatment Application:
10 Tips to Connect With the "Energetic Essence" of Others

1. Listen deeply.

2. Recognize that everyone is a teacher.

3. Come from a place of curiosity.

4. Look for the story.

5. Suspend or withhold judgment.

6. Let go of control.

7. Put down your defenses.

8. Silence your critic.

9. Realize it's not about you.

10. Find what you appreciate and acknowledge contribution. Notice and acknowledge what is happening in the room.

Treatment Application:
Presence: Minimizers and Maximizers

10 Presence MAXIMIZERS	10 Presence MINIMIZERS
Bring your full attention and focus to the person/people you are with.	Look around or at your smart phone when with others; engage in distracted multi-tasking.
Believe that everyone has something to teach you and that you can learn from everyone.	Believe you know most things and can only learn from peers, those above you in stature, and known experts.
Genuinely smile and appreciate your interaction with someone, regardless of its topic or nature.	Act hurried and feel as though you don't have time for certain people or conversations.
Be grounded, calm, and relaxed wherever you are.	Look frantic, hurried, and frazzled as you move from one thing to another.
Focus on the person you are with.	Focus on yourself, how you sound, and what you will say next.
Neat, polished, intentional grooming and appearance appropriate for your situation and role.	Sloppy, haphazard grooming with little or no attention to detail or socio-cultural role messaging.
Withhold judgment of others and realize everyone has a different perspective and orientation.	Mentally dismiss people if they don't immediately meet your credibility standards or you don't agree with them.
Demonstrate authentic respect of yourself, your body, and others by staying centered, healthy, curious, and empathetic.	Focus on polishing your outward appearance only; fake interest in others to obtain popularity, something you need, or followership.
Silence the noise and self-doubt in your mind.	Become paralyzed by rushing thoughts and anxiety from self-criticism.
Feel comfortable in your own skin and with the unique contributions you bring.	Compare yourself to others and try to be like someone else.

Ailment #1: Robot Syndrome

Leadership Remedy:
Connection—Stay Plugged In

Treatment Plan:

* Presence
* **Purpose**
* Proficiency
* People

Prognosis:
Advice Following Treatment

"What a gloomy thing, not to know the address of one's own soul." (Victor Hugo)

Robot Syndrome Treatment Plan: *Purpose*

Summary

This part of the Robot Syndrome treatment plan is designed to help you identify your unique contribution and strengths so you can hone your purpose and bring it forth in service to others. When you are grounded and act with purpose and confidence, you can connect with others more readily without feeling threatened or unworthy.

Goal

To get grounded and secure in your own unique contribution.

Real-World Scenario: Do You Know "Diane?"

Diane was promoted recently to a mid-level executive position in the marketing department of a large insurance company.

Diane is known for getting things done and for doing the work no one else wants to do. She seems to work endless hours, is tirelessly persistent, and detail-oriented. She does what's needed, when it's needed, and has been rewarded with a string of promotions to higher leadership positions.

As a leader, Diane feels the need to know everything and tell everyone what he or she should be doing. She finds delegating difficult. She is uncomfortable not knowing all the answers and has trouble letting her staff give briefings or take lead on projects. Deep down, she worries that if her staff can handle something without her, why would they need her?

Diane's over-willingness to please and need to be indispensable masks a deeper insecurity she has about the nature and value of her personal contribution.

Contribution

Each of us has a contribution to make to the world. We often refer to them as talents, gifts, or special abilities.

Regardless of how we label them, we all have things we are good at and are passionate about doing. In particular, we may have one or two things that not only are we exceptionally good at doing, but that light us up when we do them. When we contribute this gift, we feel a sense of fulfillment and purpose—as though what we are doing makes a difference and has an impact.

Part of a healthy sense of self and ego development comes from feeling as though we are making meaningful contributions to the world. Purpose grounds us and fuels our sense of confidence and significance, which are critical components of a secure sense of self. As leaders, a sense of purpose and contribution complements our presence and gives us a strong center from which to direct our energy and actions.

Figuring out what we uniquely contribute and the nature of our unique strengths are fundamental to fueling our sense of purpose.

What is your Signature Dish?

Have you ever been to a potluck party? Everyone brings a dish of food to complete the meal.

If life is one big potluck party, what dish are you bringing?

Each of us has a unique contribution to make to the world and to those around us, whether we realize it or not. This "dish" we bring to the party is the fuel of our passion. It's what makes our connector wire go "live." It's what helps us keep focused.

Trying to make too many dishes for a potluck is exhausting. On the other hand, just going to the store and picking up whatever you can find is efficient, but isn't really unique to you. That's just managing.

If you're serious about leading, then you're going to have to figure out your signature dish. Once you do, then you must declare what you're bringing and bring that dish to the party each and every moment.

Not sure what your signature dish is? Not even sure you have a dish? (Don't start with the "I'm not a good cook" excuse. You get where we're going here. Work with me.)

Your signature dish need not be grandiose. You don't need to save the world, cure cancer, or invent a perpetual motion machine. Your signature dish could be as simple as bringing others joy or keeping things focused and organized—or it could be big. The important thing is that it's your contribution, the one core thing that no matter what you are doing, or where, you can bring that forward like no one else can.

Whether you are with your kids or at work or wherever, this is the one strength and/or unique gift you contribute with energy and gusto anywhere and everywhere.

What is it?

Treatment Application:
Identifying Your Signature Dish

Answer the following:

1. What activity gives you the most energy and joy?

2. What about the experience gives you that energy and joy?

3. What is something that you just "can't help yourself" from doing? (*Think of something you do automatically and get excited about. Examples are giving people advice, telling people what to do, reading, getting involved in organizations, teaching others how to do things, organizing things, etc.*)

4. If you could do and be anything you wanted, what would you do or be? Why? What is it about that that excites you?

5. What are you most passionate about? Why?

6. What are you really good at? (*Don't say "nothing." That is not an acceptable answer.*)

7. What were you naturally good at as a child?

8. If you asked other people around you what you were good at and what your strengths are, what would they say? (*For this one, feel free to ask others to give you feedback.*)

Look at your answers. Do you notice a theme? Find the commonality and answer this final question:

What is the overarching contribution or energy you bring to others no matter what you are doing? In other words, what is your signature dish?

Now sum it up by stating the essence of who you are and the signature dish you bring to the party. Complete this sentence:

I bring _____ to the party of life.

Some examples might include:

- I bring teaching to the party of life.

- I bring warmth to the party of life.

- I bring structure and organization...

- I bring laughter and merriment...

- I bring stories...

- I bring transformation…

- I bring nurturing…

- I bring wisdom…

- I bring music…

- I bring healing…

Your Action

When you have completed your unique sentence, practice saying it to yourself. At first, this may seem weird, but ignore that feeling and just say the sentence again and own it for yourself. Are you bringing your signature dish every day and in every encounter?

Write your sentence down and post it somewhere conspicuous so you can see it.

Repeat the sentence to yourself every morning and make a conscious effort to bring this dish with you. Don't just show up to the party empty-handed or just pick up anything convenient along the way. This dish is part of your signature brand as a person and as a leader.

None of us brings quite the same dishes prepared in quite the same ways. If you are clear about your signature dish and bring it with you to every party, you will start to perfect the recipe. You will cease comparing your dish to the dishes of others and will find ways to embellish and perfect it. You will start to feel more comfortable in your own skin and with what you bring to the table. You will become clearer about what you uniquely contribute . . . and that secretly held "NGE" (Not Good Enough) factor will disappear.

Ailment #1: Robot Syndrome

Leadership Remedy:
Connection—Stay Plugged In

Treatment Plan:

- Presence
- Purpose
- **Proficiency**
- People

Prognosis:
Advice Following Treatment

"Leadership and learning are indispensable to each other." (John F. Kennedy)

Robot Syndrome Treatment Plan: *Proficiency*

Summary

Being competent and proficient is critical to our credibility as leaders. Yet "knowing it all" can also create blind, exclusive models in our minds that we use to filter information; not allowing us to be open to new ways of doing things and limiting innovation. To combat Robot Syndrome and stay connected, we must see our proficiency as not only our current competence level, but as our ability to stay open, be curious, unlearn, and continuously relearn what we think we already know with a beginner's mind.

Goal

To be a perpetual learner.

Real-World Scenario: Do You Know "Kevin?"

I recently began a coaching engagement with "Kevin," a leader considered technically brilliant by everyone who knows him. Recently, Kevin moved out of an executive level role, where he had been for four years, to a senior manager role.

Feedback precipitating the move said Kevin was "unable to adapt to the changing customer requirements and outside forces influencing the direction of the company" and that his behavior indicated he was "too stuck in his ways" to think differently and be innovative.

Kevin takes pride in being an expert in his area. He tells everyone the right way to do things, and bristles when people use technical terms for the wrong application. He is convinced there are right ways and wrong ways to implement things, and that those who are familiar with his field know the difference.

Unfortunately for Kevin, most people don't care about or understand the technical differences he focuses on. They care about achieving results and his insistence on differentiating terminology and technical jargon works against him.

By focusing so much on being technically right, he is unable to translate his technical competence into a model or words that others can understand and use. He also limits his own ideas of how the work should be done to what the experts say, rather than trying to transcend what is known and create new and different applications for the future.

Confidence and Self

Being "good" at something fuels our confidence, which forms over time as we experience repeated successes, reinforcement, and achievement. When we feel successful at something, acknowledged by others, and sought out to apply our expertise and achieve a goal, we become more self-assured in our abilities. Feedback and positive reinforcement helps us feel valued and meaningful, and that our contributions have an impact.

Over time our ego, or sense of self, gets wrapped around being proficient at something—and the more we know about something, and the more we are able to achieve, the greater this sense of self grows.

Sometimes our ego grows to a degree that it clouds our ability to learn or take in new information. We begin to think we "know it all" and consider only those who are more proficient to be credible sources of knowledge and continued learning.

Proficiency is a double-edged sword: being good at something and achieving success is critical to developing our sense of self; being competent and being viewed as competent by others is essential to our credibility as leaders; and feeling confident with our proficiency and continuously learning is a big contributor to this overall credibility. Yet, part of the fragility of expertise is that it comes with an expiration date. What we know for sure today may be obsolete tomorrow. Just when we think we know it all, the world changes and there we are, stuck in our old ways of thinking based on our brilliant expertise.

As we strive for expertise and achievement, we must remain open to new and continuous learning from practically everywhere, anytime.

The mental models we create about how things are and what they should be like become fixed and stagnant when we don't allow new data from varied sources to meld with and deconstruct old ideas to create ever-evolving new ones.

Being too stuck on proficiency influences the Robot Syndrome:

- There is one way to give presentations.

- There is one way to interact in a meeting.

- There is one way to do things around here.

As we become proficient at making sure we do it that "one way," innovation, authenticity, and creativity get squashed, as does the human connection.

An open mind, a zest for continuous learning, and a propensity to unlearn and relearn are the best routes to gaining and maintaining flexible proficiency.

Treatment Application:
Proficiency: Questions to Ask Yourself

Answer the following:

1. Are you competent in your job?

2. Do you spend time maintaining your proficiency in the areas that are most important to your success?

3. Do you ask questions as much as you "tell"?

4. Do you make snap judgments about people and information based on what you think you "already know?"

5. How do the current "mental models" you have in your head about what are the "right" ways inhibit your learning?

6. Do you try to learn something from everyone and everything, or only from those you deem to be smarter than or as capable as you are?

7. With things constantly changing, how do you know your current ways of looking at things aren't becoming outdated?

8. What unconventional things have you tried?

9. Are your networks broad and diverse or closed and homogeneous?

Treatment Application:
10 Tips for Continuous Learning

1. Approach things with a beginner's mind.

2. Learn something from everyone.

3. Listen and observe more than or at least as much as you talk.

4. Read as much as possible.

5. Expand your social networks.

6. Attend conferences/workshops in your specialty area.

7. Keep abreast of the latest developments in your industry and domain of expertise.

8. Be curious and ask questions.

9. Be open to different ideas and views.

10. Don't be afraid to look stupid or fail.

Ailment #1: Robot Syndrome

Leadership Remedy:
Connection—Stay Plugged In

Treatment Plan:

- Presence
- Purpose
- Proficiency
- **People**

Prognosis:
Advice Following Treatment

"By appreciation we make excellence in others our own property." (Voltaire)

Robot Syndrome Treatment Plan: *People*

Summary

Being able to see, value, and appreciate others is a critical part of real connection, and absolutely essential for combatting Robot Syndrome. If you are focused only on yourself, your "self-consciousness" doesn't allow you to transcend your own ego and learn from and connect with other people. The ability to do this is critical if you want to "plug in" and engage others.

Goal

To value and appreciate the contributions of others.

Real-World Scenario: Do You Know "Darryl?"

Results and impressions don't always equate to good people leadership. For example, Darryl has been on the fast track in his organization since day one. Smart, polished, articulate, and a smooth talker, he has said all the right things to all the right people. He is a master networker who delivers results. His bosses love him, and the impression he has made on the senior executives in the organization is stellar. They view him as someone with the "highest potential" to take on a senior executive role in the future.

Recently, Darryl was the focus of a 360-feedback employee engagement survey. His results were unexpected. Comments from Darryl's direct reports painted a contradictory picture on his presumed leadership potential. Common descriptors included "intimidating and abrasive," "controlling and uncaring," and "self-centered and self-absorbed."

When presented with his feedback, Darryl brashly dismissed it as being due to his courage to "hold people accountable" and to his direct reports' lack of ingenuity, thought leadership, and ability to innovate.

In his mind, Darryl sees himself as the change agent and his direct reports are merely stuck in their dysfunctional, non-productive ways. He is there to "save the day" and implement cutting edge solutions. Someone has to do it, he insists, and he is happy to be that person.

Your Healthy Self

Part of developing a healthy sense of self is to be secure enough in your own abilities to transcend your ego. This means not feeling a need to be perceived as the smartest, highest-achieving, or highest status person in the room to confirm your own value.

A big contributor to Robot Syndrome is a leader's need for validation and for everything to be about his or her success and achievement. When a leader's need for personal validation, achievement, and success is high, he or she is left with little room to validate and appreciate others, except in terms of how it contributes to his or her own needs.

I remember a senior leader who was known in her organization as the "Queen Bee." Those around her knew they needed to stroke her ego and tell her how marvelous she was on a regular basis to get rewarded, while those who gave her honest feedback or offered contributions considered different from hers or innovative were banished—as such contributions were not hers.

Queen Bee had built the organization so she was the clear centerpiece, and everyone knew it. Her own insecurities and need for constant validation created a dysfunctional, albeit temporarily productive, organizational dynamic. The ailments of Robot Syndrome and Yes-itis (which we will cover later), were in full force. The mode of operating was for everyone to tell the Queen what she wanted to hear—to protect the her fragile sense of self above all else.

When you are grounded in your own presence, clear about your own purpose and contribution, and comfortable with your own proficiency and continuous learning, your sense of security allows you to move from a focus on self to a focus on communion with others. You see others as people with unique talents and gifts. You honor and draw out their contributions by showing them genuine appreciation and validation.

This is a critical component of people leadership, and it's why the deep work you do on developing your sense of self is so essential to being a good leader.

The ability to connect with others at a deep level is only possible when you come from a secure, genuine, non-threatened place within. If you truly don't care about other people and are only focused on your own agenda, goals, contributions, and success, then plugging in the "connector cord" and engaging other people is impossible. If your energy is completely self-absorbed and self-conscious, there is no way to connect it to anything except for your own self-encompassing thoughts.

Treatment Application:
People: Questions to Ask Yourself

Answer the following:

1. Are you genuinely interested in others and their contributions or do you see people only in terms of what they can offer you?

2. When talking to others, are you fully focused on them and what they are saying?

3. Do you find yourself usually judging others as they talk to you, and filtering the information through the judgment you have formed?

4. Do you listen openly, with curiosity, and without an agenda?

5. Do you constantly compare yourself to others in interactions?

6. Are you as comfortable acknowledging and celebrating the successes of others as much as your own?

7. Do you spend more time looking for validation or more time looking to validate others?

8. Do you look for the "feeling" tone in a conversation and empathize with the other person's perspective and feelings?

9. Do you find value in every person you encounter?

Treatment Application:
10 Tips for Connecting with People

1. Approach each person with curiosity and interest.

2. See past the facades and focus on the strengths.

3. Believe that every person has something to contribute.

4. Withhold your judgment and evaluation and don't mentally dismiss the person's value to you.

5. Give your full attention and listen fully.

6. Stand in the other person's shoes.

7. Focus on the person and his or her story—not on yourself.

8. Acknowledge and show appreciation.

9. Respect, accept, and honor differences.

10. Show empathy.

Ailment #1: Robot Syndrome

Leadership Remedy:
Connection—Stay Plugged In

Treatment Plan:

- Presence
- Purpose
- Proficiency
- People

Prognosis:
Advice Following Treatment

Robot Syndrome Prognosis: *Advice Following Treatment*

Robot Syndrome is a potent ailment that spreads like an epidemic in many organizations.

As a leader—the one who sets the energetic tone for your organization and models the accepted and unspoken behaviors for others to emulate—you are the main carrier of this silent disease without even knowing it.

Robot Syndrome sneaks up slowly. Most often, you don't even realize you have it. You are operating in an unconscious state, dutifully complying with what you think is protocol and accepted standards.

Soon you embody and reinforce de-humanizing procedures and behaviors, and the human cord of real connection unplugs. You lose the human element in your organization, and the initiatives you put in place to get it back just don't work.

If you are serious about ridding your organization of this lethal and potent ailment, a genuine soul-searching of yourself as a leader, with a focus on the four "P"s in the Robot Syndrome treatment plan will take you there:

- *Presence*—Take time to examine your own presence as a leader and how connected you are to the deepest part of yourself. This is fundamental to grounding yourself in a secure place and letting go of your own insecurities and reactive tendencies.

- *Purpose*—Determine what you uniquely contribute and what you bring to the table to heighten your sense of confidence and connectedness, and become even more grounded and secure. Acting with clear and intentional purpose is a powerful platform from which to stand and connect to others.

- ***Proficiency***—Being and feeling competent is a foundational part of your credibility as a leader and an entry point into being heard by others. However, proficiency comes not only from personal competence, but from continuous learning and being open and curious without getting stuck in mental models of how things are/should be.

- ***People***—Truly connecting with the deep human element in people is not the same as just telling others what to do. Without genuinely valuing and appreciating the contribution of others and forging that connection to a deeper place inside them, you cannot achieve real engagement. Having a live wire and plugging the magic cord of connection into those around you only comes from sincerely valuing our inherent commonalities and appreciating differences and perspectives.

When you follow the treatments and apply them over time, the Robot Syndrome slowly dissipates.

Robot Syndrome is a tricky ailment, though, and is prone to relapse. Staying grounded, open, present, and secure—regardless of the winds of everyday dramas roaring around you—requires constant diligence and effort.

As a reminder to stay on course, think of yourself as a solid, strong, well-rooted redwood tree—impervious to the daily weather and connected deep in the ground by an unbreakable, unmovable root system.

Ailment #2: "In No One We Trust" Toxicity

Can You Be Trusted?

Think back to the first job you had. What behaviors made you either trust or distrust your boss? Development of trust in the workplace is simple . . . but vitally important to your ability to lead others.

When it comes to the companies for which we've worked and their leaders, most reading this book have experienced some level of trust or distrust.

Repeated interactions send us messages about whether or not we should trust the behaviors we see and the words we hear. When we receive mixed messages, inconsistent signals and behaviors—when our leaders say one thing and do another, when they change direction frequently or reveal contradictory agendas—as employees, we have no option but to feel distrustful. "I hear what you're saying, but I'm not sure I believe you" becomes the unspoken and underlying sentiment.

Prolonged exposure to this sentiment results in "In No One We Trust" toxicity, which is rampant in many organizations. Because of internal politics, leadership posturing, reorganizations, layoffs, poor communication, operating in silos, hidden agendas, personal insecurities, feelings of threat, under-the-covers maneuvering, and surprise announcements, people lose trust in the companies that employ them and in the leaders who lead them.

They come to believe that what is stated is one thing, while how things work and what really happens is quite another . . . and the more things seem secretive, unspoken, and hidden, the more the toxicity permeates. The toxicity borders on lethal, as it poisons interactions, initiatives, authenticity, productivity, and discretionary effort.

If I don't trust you, I don't have respect for you. If I don't have respect for you, then I am likely to withhold information, ideas, effort, and genuine interaction. I "go through the motions," but the sense of threat I feel is always in the background, resulting in fear. When I operate from fear, I become defensive, reactive, protective, or tend to over please to get along. In this state of "fight or flight" sensitivity, the organization stalls and maximum creative and productive capability is impossible to achieve.

Trust is nebulous and hard to define. We learn about trust all our lives, from early experiences with caregivers, our parents, friends, and all the people we encounter. We learn what is safe and what isn't, where we can let our guard down and relax, and where we must use our primal instincts to discern danger and be prepared for a fight or flight response. When we don't have trust in something or someone, a primitive part of our brain takes over and puts us on high alert to protect us and ensure survival.

When lack of trust prevails in an organization, people worry about survival more than everything else. This kind of environment is toxic. Employees either feel uneasy and on guard, as though they are in constant danger, unable to pinpoint exactly what is wrong; or they feel lethargic and numb, almost zombie-like. In either case, employees simply go through the motions, with little or no personal investment in outcomes. They work to get a paycheck.

Where, Oh Where is the Trust?

Most company leaders want to be trusted and feel as though they are trustworthy. When engagement and ethics surveys and other feedback mechanisms indicate low trust in a department or entire organization, leaders are often perplexed. "How can this be?" They wonder. "It must be due to the next management level's lack of skills." (More on this later in *Ailment #4: Blame Disorder.*)

Trust doesn't form or erode instantly. Lack of trust results from the perception of a threat due to one bad experience or consistent behaviors over time.

I have observed and concluded from years of working with, watching, and talking to thousands of leaders in organizations, that one of the main culprits causing lack of trust is the lack of authenticity in leadership.

What is Authenticity?

The word authenticity comes from the Greek word meaning "original" or "from original form."

Being authentic isn't just about being truthful or honest—it comes from being connected to that place in your deepest self that we talked about in Robot Syndrome. When you are authentic, you come from that pure, whole, and transparent place without manifesting fear- and insecurity-fueled behaviors designed to protect, control, please, or put on airs to impress others.

When you are authentic, you are comfortable in your own skin. You have no need to protect yourself. You don't feel threatened. You are connected to the deepest part of yourself and are able to connect to the deepest part of others. Interactions occur in good faith and without hidden agendas. Your intent is pure. You are fully present.

What is "In No One We Trust" Toxicity?

"In No One We Trust" Toxicity is an organizational toxic environment characterized by lack of trust and the perception of secret, hidden maneuvering. It builds over time and is a result of an absence of authenticity in communication and interaction. It usually presents itself with Robot Syndrome.

Common Symptoms

- Assume the worst intentions and motives for actions/behaviors without trying to validate assumptions or give benefit of the doubt

- Fear of retribution if a contrary opinion or question is offered; stay quiet rather than seem to dissent or disagree

- Believe everyone is viewed as a disposable commodity to be used until not needed

- Low personal investment of voluntary discretionary effort except when coerced or in fear mode

- Fake a persona rather than express your true self

- Climate of change with seemingly hidden activities and little or no communication about them and/or no or few updates during changes

Contributing Factors

The following leadership behaviors contribute to the development of "In No One We Trust" Toxicity:

- Lack of or poor regular and timely communication

- "Cloak and daggers" messaging that indicates hidden, non-communicated, behind-the-scenes maneuvering and planning

- Ostracizing, ignoring, removing, or disapproving of someone who expresses a deferring opinion or question

- Reactive, last minute actions aimed to correct or cover up perceived problems

- Saying one thing yet doing another

- Couching negative or unpopular messages with positive platitudes or cryptic language

- Changing point of view depending on what the higher "boss" says, or having no point of view—lack of a "backbone"

- Fear to push back on or disagree with leaders higher up the organization

- Failure to listen to, acknowledge, understand, and show care about the welfare, concerns, or opinions of others

- Spending little time with employees and most of your time in more "important" meetings behind closed doors

- Staying intensely private and not sharing any personal information to show you are human and have a real life outside of work just like everyone else

- Neglecting to ask about or show genuine care about the lives, interests, and aspirations of others

- Maintaining an aura of authority and positional status with strict protocols for how people lower in the organization may communicate with you

- Ousting those who tell you the truth or give you feedback you dislike

---

Main Cause of "In No One We Trust" Toxicity:

Absence of Authenticity

"IN NO ONE WE TRUST" TOXICITY
Leadership Remedy & Treatment Plan

If your organization is afflicted with "In No One We Trust" Toxicity, your actions and behaviors as a leader are creating the toxins. Once these toxins are released and the toxicity is rampant, ridding the organization of impure air is difficult.

Only by committing to a rigorous treatment plan and acknowledging what has contributed to the contamination, can you exterminate the toxicity and purify the air. Doing so takes consistency, diligence, commitment, honesty, and a great dose of humility. Only serious commitment to role modeling the three components outlined in this treatment plan will enable long-term maintenance, free of the dangerous toxins.

A Word of Caution: As soon as you revert to old behaviors, the toxins will come back. Consistency of behavior and action is paramount. The application of treatment must be real; your behaviors cannot be faked. After all, lack of authenticity is what caused the toxins in the first place—and people can easily discern between authentic behavior and manipulation.

You must do the deep work on yourself to enable these behaviors. See the treatment plan for Robot Syndrome before you begin this treatment. If you are suffering from Robot Syndrome, you must treat and eliminate that ailment first before treating this one or else this treatment will not work.

Ailment #2: "In No One We Trust" Toxicity

Leadership Remedy:
Authenticity—Open Your Kimono

Treatment Plan:

- Transparency
- Tact
- Touch

Prognosis:
Advice Following Treatment

"In No One We Trust" Toxicity Leadership Remedy: *Authenticity—Open Your Kimono*

The *Leadership Remedy* for "In No One We Trust" Toxicity is Authenticity.

The *Treatment Plan* consists of consists of three components—Transparency, Tact, and Touch—that will help increase your authenticity and begin to eliminate toxicity from your organization.

Transparency

Your actions, words, and intentions are open, communicated, and in alignment without hidden agendas.

Tact

You choose your words empathetically to take into account and show understanding of the feelings of others and their potential perspectives and reactions.

Touch

You genuinely care about the feelings of others and their potential perspectives and reactions and spend time acknowledging your understanding of them. You connect with people at a deeper level, listen intently, and visibly show compassion, empathy, and concern.

Ailment #2: "In No One We Trust" Toxicity

Leadership Remedy:
Authenticity—Open Your Kimono

Treatment Plan:

- Transparency
- Tact
- Touch

Prognosis:
Advice Following Treatment

"In No One We Trust" Toxicity: *Transparency*

Summary

Telling people what is happening, stating openly when you can't talk about something, and communicating frequently without a hidden agenda are all essential to being more transparent. Transparency is the foundation and breeding ground for trust to begin to grow. Without it, trust erodes and decreases. In order to be more authentic, you must communicate and behave more transparently.

Goal

To communicate your intentions openly so that others clearly know what to expect.

Real-World Scenario: Do you Know "Karen?"

Karen is the Vice-President of an 800-employee Human Resources organization in a global Fortune 500 hotel services company.

Due to lagging growth in key markets and the sluggish profit margins of some of their traditional brands, the company's new strategy is to rebrand, consolidate, and reorganize. This presents an opportunity to leverage the strategic role of HR in workforce planning, talent management, organizational effectiveness, and leadership development. To do this, Karen must do the same rebranding and reorganizing of her own HR organization.

She is worried about the implications that word of a potential reorganization will have on the levels of service and productivity. "If everyone's attention becomes focused on the reorganization," she rationalizes, "then no work will get done."

She hires a consultant to help her design and rebrand the organization, and spends months behind closed doors planning the changes. When asked in meetings if the company's overall new strategy will affect the

HR organization, she is evasive and indirect. She figures why discuss the rebranding effort when it is only half-baked?

Seeing is Believing

Glass is transparent. If you look at it, you can see right through it. You know what is there. What you see is what you get. Things that aren't transparent are either harder or impossible to see through. You're not sure what is inside. What you see may not be what you get.

- "Is it safe?"

- "Will it hurt me?"

- "Will it change without me knowing?"

These fundamental questions must be answered when you can't see what's behind the glass, otherwise you won't be able to relax and trust or make decisions from a place of knowing. After all, things might be happening back there that you can't see. There could be a tiger poised to pounce . . . or there could be nothing at all.

When you can't see, when you can't know, when there's no transparency, evaluating a situation and your options is virtually impossible. You can't possibly know whether you should run or stand pat.

Transparency plays to our basic animal survival instincts. It allows us to gauge our own safety.

The Transparency Dilemma

As a leader trying to rid your organization of "In No One We Trust" Toxicity and become more transparent, you face some real dynamic dilemmas.

How can you be more transparent when the nature of how organizations operate tends to induce political maneuvering and secrecy?

Leaders often feel torn. There are things they feel they can't tell everyone, such as proprietary information that can't be shared freely. There are also conversations about people and promotions and a host of other details that leaders are privy to that just can't be shared for a variety of reasons.

Not surprisingly, the more of these things there are in an organization, the more secretive its leadership appears—the more the "tiger" pops out from behind the rock with no warning, and the more afraid and distrustful of their environment employees become.

The more open leaders can be about what they're doing and why they can't share some or all information, the more transparent they will be.

Transparency doesn't mean you have to spill all the beans and tell everyone about everything all the time (in fact, you shouldn't do that). Transparency is about being up front about a situation, your intentions, and communicating openly.

The more people see that behavior from you, the leader, the more comfortable they will feel about your intentions and the more likely they will be to exhibit the same behavior you are modeling.

Treatment Application:
Examples of Transparent Vs. Non-Transparent Behaviors

TRANSPARENT	NON-TRANSPARENT
Sharing appropriate, real, personal information about yourself; allowing others to see your human vulnerabilities	Sharing no personal information about yourself; sharing no human vulnerabilities and maintaining a persona of detachment and perfection
Openly acknowledging mistakes	Hiding mistakes
Apologizing when wrong	Refusing to apologize when wrong, blaming others
Communicating openly and often	Communicating on a "need-to-know" basis only
Sharing information	Withholding information
Answering questions directly	Evading questions
Being able to laugh at yourself	Taking yourself too seriously
Assuming most people are basically trustworthy	Assuming that most people are out to get you and staying guarded
Stating your feelings	Hiding your feelings
Clearly stating what you want	Keeping others guessing or trying to figure out what you want

Treatment Application:
Increasing Transparency: Questions to ask Yourself

1. Do you let people know what you are thinking and feeling, or do you usually keep those things hidden?

2. Do you honestly let people know when you are feeling confused or don't know the answers?

3. Do you regularly share personal facts and information about yourself with others?

4. Do you show your human side by admitting mistakes and showing vulnerability?

5. Do you share information with others regularly or keep it hidden and close to the vest?

6. Do you communicate with others openly?

7. Do you tell people openly when and why you cannot share information with them?

Treatment Application:
10 Tips to Increasing Transparency

1. Show that you are human by sharing some personal things with people about your life outside of work.

2. Admit when you don't have the answers and ask for help.

3. Communicate what you know and what you can share frequently and regularly, and not just on a need-to-know basis.

4. When you are making a change or anticipate a change, tell people what is happening and why.

5. Be honest with people when you can't share information, telling them that you can't share and why.

6. Communicate to others your expectations and what you want clearly and openly.

7. Show others that you don't have a hidden agenda by expressing your motives.

8. Show trust in others by assuming that they are trustworthy and giving them the benefit of the doubt.

9. Laugh at yourself and don't take yourself too seriously.

10. Admit when you are wrong or make a mistake.

Ailment #2: "In No One We Trust" Toxicity

Leadership Remedy:
Authenticity—Open Your Kimono

Treatment Plan:

- Transparency
- Tact
- Touch

Prognosis:
Advice Following Treatment

"Tact is the art of making a point without making an enemy." (Isaac Newton)

"In No One We Trust" Toxicity: *Tact*

Summary

The use of tact in relating with others is a critical part of being authentic. Tact involves being able to tune into another person's emotions, discerning his or her tone and perspective, and then adjusting the delivery of your message to acknowledge that understanding.

Goal

To show understanding and empathy for the feelings and perspectives of other people.

Real World Example: Do You Know "Colleen?"

Colleen is a general manager in a large media company. With the boom of the internet and social media, traditional advertising mediums and venues the company once relied on to bring in revenue are becoming obsolete. Her team is under a lot of pressure to get ahead of the future and bring in new and creative revenue streams. Colleen understands that if the company and even her own job are to survive, she and her team must think of innovative and new ways of garnering business.

Colleen is feeling anxious. Her new team was hired to think of new ways to approach old paradigms, and she thinks the presentations and ideas they have come up with so far have been lukewarm.

Most team meetings end with her telling the group their ideas are off the mark and/or just plain dumb. She reminds them that their jobs are at stake if they don't come up with what they were hired to do and she questions aloud whether they are the right people for the assignment.

When questioned about her bluntness, Colleen insists she is merely trying to invoke a sense of fear and urgency in the team. "I have to be honest and authentic," she contends. "They need to know they are not hitting the mark."

It's Not Only What You Say; It's How You Say It

Being authentic isn't about saying whatever pops into your head. For others to receive your message and hear what you are saying, you must be skilled in the use of tact.

Tact is the ability to tune into another person's sensitivities and feelings so you can discern how to deliver a message that does not offend. Beware, though, being tactful does not mean not being truthful, nor does it mean couching things so that they are always positive. Being tactful means picking up on and understanding the "feeling tones" in an interaction, empathizing with those unspoken feelings, and framing your message to acknowledge and account for those feelings in your delivery.

Transparency, as we discussed earlier, is important, but without tact, transparency is self-centered. Tact shows you have empathy, that you value what the person is bringing forward whether you agree with it or not, and that you want to maintain the relationship.

The use of tact acknowledges that you care to preserve the other person's dignity and self-esteem in an exchange with you. This allows for emotional safety which, as we discussed earlier, is a key component of trust.

For example, if I trust that the exchange we are having is not a reflection of my low value or worth in your eyes, I am more apt to trust you and not take anything you say personally. However, if the interaction establishes you as *superior* and me as *inferior* in worth, I will walk away feeling unsafe around you.

In essence, tact is emotional assurance—or even better, emotional insurance. Tact is the personalized de-personalizing glue that allows for transparency in an interaction without alienating or denigrating the other person with a message.

Treatment Application:
Examples of Tactful Vs. Tactless Behaviors

TACTFUL	TACTLESS
Thinking of the impact on the other person before you speak	Blurting out whatever comes to mind without regard of its impact on another
Discerning the feeling tone underneath an interaction and adjusting accordingly	Ignoring or being oblivious to the feeling tone in an interaction
Acknowledging another perspective	Ignoring or dismissing perspectives other than your own
Trying to create a win/win interaction	Focusing the interaction on you being "right"
Preserving the self-esteem of the other person in the interaction	Disregarding the self-esteem of the other person and insisting on brutal "honesty"
Maintaining respect for the other person at all times	Maintaining being "right" at all costs
Maintaining the relationship while voicing your opinion	Voicing your opinion with no regard for the impact on the relationship
Using non-inflammatory language	Using provocative and potentially inflammatory language
Avoiding blaming the other person	Assigning blame to the other person
Screening your own views for biases, judgments, or potential intolerance	Expressing your views without filtering for your own biases, judgments, intolerance, or impact on others

Treatment Application:
Increasing Your Tactfulness: Questions to Ask Yourself

1. Before I blurt out the emotion I feel, do I pause and think about how the message will be received?

2. Do I think of ways to phrase my comment so that it is both truthful AND acknowledges the other person's value?

3. Does my comment maintain the other person's self-esteem and dignity?

4. Is my tone superior or am I relaying the message as an equal?

5. Am I caught up in my own personal judgments and emotions?

6. Do I articulate that my comment is not a personal attack and clarify my intentions?

7. Am I in tune with my own insecurities and emotional triggers? Do I self-manage them?

8. Do I tune into the other person's feelings and acknowledge their existence?

Ailment #2: "In No One We Trust" Toxicity

Leadership Remedy: Authenticity—Open Your Kimono

Treatment Plan:

* Transparency
* Tact
* Touch

Prognosis: Advice Following Treatment

"A human being is a part of the whole called by us universe, a part limited in time and space. He experiences himself, his thoughts and feeling as something separated from the rest, a kind of optical delusion of his consciousness. This delusion is a kind of prison for us, restricting us to our personal desires and to affection for a few persons nearest to us. Our task must be to free ourselves from this prison by widening our circle of compassion to embrace all living creatures and the whole of nature in its beauty." (Albert Einstein)

"In No One We Trust" Toxicity: *Touch*

Summary

Connecting at a deep level, listening intently, and visibly showing compassion, empathy, and concern are all essential components of connecting to people and increasing "touch." Touch is essential to building trust with human beings.

Goal

To connect with others at a deep level, listen intently, and visibly show compassion, empathy, and concern.

Real World Example: Do You Know "Carl?"

Carl was hired a year ago as the Senior Vice President of Marketing for a large conglomerate media company with a staff of more 1,000 marketing professionals around the world. The company's CEO tasked Carl to reengineer and retool all marketing functions and create a new operating model to best support current strategy and talent needs.

Much of the existing staff had "grown up" in the company, rising through the ranks with little or no training or expertise in business development or marketing. The current structure was decentralized and scattered, with different processes at different locations and much duplication of effort.

Carl imagined the redesign would save money and help revitalize and refocus critical functions. It would also help identify and leverage top marketing talent across the company, and highlight opportunities where new talent and essential expertise might be needed.

Carl hired a consultant to work the redesign and he kept the staff informed along the way. When he finally announced the new model, to no one's surprise, he communicated all of the information crisply, logically, and thoroughly. The story he told was true and made perfect sense for the company. Objective business people, whether they liked the model or not, had to agree it was the right thing for the company. Most in the department, even those negatively affected, agreed with it as well. They did not all care for the changes, and some feared for their futures, but the recommendations made sense in the big picture.

Carl seemed to follow the script of what a leader should do to lead such a major change effort. He had the fortitude, courage, and communication down pat. Yet there was something missing from his process and the communication.

Others sensed a tone in the way Carl was operating that permeated and negated much of what he was saying. Employees characterized his delivery as "icy" and "soulless," lacking warmth and personal connection. He seemed to have formed a high-level, sweeping impression of everyone, and those who heard him sensed a superior tone in his message. Throughout the process, he made no effort to connect with any of the affected employees or get to know them.

Undoubtedly, Carl was in the grip of Robot Syndrome, and his lack of connection and his presence silenced his message. All people walked away with was the feeling, "You don't care about me—I am just a resource. I don't trust you."

The commitment Carl so needed to build for this effort had, in fact, quickly turned to sheer compliance fueled by fear.

Your Heart Speaks Louder Than Your Words

Authenticity is about being the purest form of yourself, without all the layers of fears, insecurities, and protective reactions we have learned over the years. It's about accessing that place deep within that realizes you are not just you, but that you are connected to everyone else on a deep level.

Presence and authenticity are intimately intertwined. In fact, your true presence is the expression of your authentic self. Your authentic self is both unique to you and at the same time a collective imprint of humanity and the entire human experience.

You may be wondering what this has to do with leadership and organizations, and how this is even remotely related to business and profitability?

Here's how: human beings create business and profitability. Humans are connected to each other at the deepest level by virtue of their humanity. We need to feel connected, valued, and understood to perform at our best. Valuing, understanding, empathizing with, and connecting to others are all part of the "touch" component in the trust-building treatment plan—the ability to show others that you genuinely care about them and their welfare.

Operating with the element of touch means you are aware of others, their contributions, and their unique value, and that you show that. It means being approachable and connecting with all, regardless of their status, function, or closeness to you. Touch connotes a sense of warmth that comes from you, and implies that you see the commonality between you and others. Genuine touch shows your heart, and allows others to see it and connect to it.

Can this be possible in a business environment? Or is this getting a bit too personal and touchy-feely? Won't this interfere with objective decision-making?

Touch has nothing to do with being overly "nice" or a pushover. It does not mean you lower performance standards or lower your job expectations. Touch relates to how you treat and connect to people.

You can be firm, fair, and even tough. That doesn't mean you can't be personable and warm, and treat others with respect. It doesn't mean you must be distant, aloof, cold, and impersonal.

Learning to show your humanity and seeing the humanity in others is an essential part of increasing your authenticity.

Treatment Application:
Behaviors that Increase and Decrease Touch

INCREASE	DECREASE
Smiling at people warmly and genuinely	Having a stone face or scowl in the presence of others
Acknowledging others' feelings	Being unaware of or unconcerned with others' feelings
Nodding your head, making eye contact, and using body language to connect with others	Averting your eyes and looking down while talking to others, maintaining a "poker face"
Acknowledging discomfort or awkwardness in situations	Ignoring discomfort and awkwardness as if they didn't exist
Showing your vulnerability	Acting superior or invincible and flaunting your authority
Listening to and valuing different perspectives without needing agreement	Dismissing perspectives that differ from your own
Asking questions to increase understanding	Telling others only what you think
Making time to talk to others	Seeing talking to others as a time waster
Staying calm when someone disagrees with you; inviting disagreement	Looking annoyed when someone disagrees with you; shunning disagreement
Showing you care by your deliberate personal choice of words	Using language that is indifferent and impersonal

Treatment Application:
Increasing Touch: Questions to Ask Yourself

1. What messages are you sending to others with your body language and facial expressions?

2. Do you convey warmth and openness, or aloofness, distance, and disapproval?

3. Are you always too busy to make time for others?

4. Do you consider listening to others a waste of time unless they have something to give you?

5. Do you ask questions to understand other perspectives or tell others why your perspective is right?

6. Do you smile when someone approaches you to show approachability or look disinterested?

7. Do you admit when you are at a loss for words?

8. Do you tell people what you appreciate about them regularly?

9. Do you show understanding and compassion for people's feelings and points of view?

Ailment #2: "In No One We Trust" Toxicity

Leadership Remedy:
Authenticity—Open Your Kimono

Treatment Plan:

- Transparency
- Tact
- Touch

Prognosis:
Advice Following Treatment

"In No One We Trust" Toxicity Prognosis: *Advice Following Treatment*

Trust is the bedrock of all relationships. Without trust in an organization, there is little commitment.

Distrust breeds acting a part and keeping things hidden rather than showing your real motives. Keeping things hidden breeds more distrust . . . and so the toxicity of distrust stays in the air as a potent part of the environment.

With diligent efforts to increase your authenticity, you can begin to purify the air. The treatment plan of transparency, tact, and touch must be internalized, and you must commit to being vulnerable and staying true to stamping out the toxins.

Pure air is fragile. Genuine commitment and continuous attention and effort is required to keep the distrust toxins at bay. It is possible to do so, but you must also be careful not to allow the Robot Syndrome to creep in—as it will cause "In No One We Trust" Toxicity to re-surface.

If you . . .

- Commit to being **transparent** and open in your interactions with others

- Use **tact** as an indicator that you are attuned to the feelings and perspectives of others, and

- Genuinely care about other people at a deeper level through the element of **touch**

. . . your chances of eliminating the deadly "In No One We Trust" Toxicity from yourself and your organization are high.

Ailment #3: Yes-itis

The Emperor Has No Clothes

Most of us like people who like us. We like it when others agree with our opinions and treat us nicely. Feeling affiliation and comfort around someone who agrees with us and appears to approve of our way of being and actions is natural. We usually approve of the person back, and see him or her favorably. We all want positive supporters and fans in our lives.

A striking phenomenon I have observed repeatedly in my work with leaders is the manifestation of Yes-itis.

Yes-itis occurs when you are the boss and everyone agrees with you all of the time.

The people around you continuously compliment you, agree with you, try to figure out what you want, or merely execute what they think they heard you say you want. Their thinking apparatus is in the "off" position, and they dare not question you or explain to you why what you want either doesn't make sense or won't work.

Their opinions mimic your opinions, because they think that's the way you want it. They are your minions, at your service, ready to serve and please. They leave their brains at the door—as it is clear to them that *you* will do all the thinking.

They consider disagreeing with you risky. They believe if they question your thinking, you'll get angry or annoyed and they will fall from your favor and graces (which is the last thing a minion wants to do!). They consider such behavior too risky—they could potentially lose their jobs and be banished from the kingdom forever.

A funny thing happens when organizations are swimming in Yes-itis toxicity. Leaders start to buy into their minions' ruse. They start to bask in the seeming adoration, and the more the minions feed them, the more they believe them and reinforce their behavior. Yes-itis becomes a potent, pervading force.

What is Yes-itis?

Yes-itis is an ailment that appears in organizations when employees are not empowered and are afraid to take risks. It manifests as over-agreeability and blind execution without questioning.

A perfect example of Yes-itis can be found in the old tale, *The Emperor Has No Clothes.* Everyone lauded whatever the emperor said and fulfilled his every wish, yet no one ever told him the truth—even when he was embarrassing himself by parading around with no clothes on!

Yes-itis is the modern-day organizational version of this story, and it is rampant in today's organizations.

Common Symptoms

- Over-eagerness to please and total agreement on comments and direction

- Lack of courage to tell an emperor/empress that he/she has no clothes on, and instead smiling at the spectacle as though it was not happening

- Fear of having or expressing an opinion or idea alternate to the prevailing thinking

- Over-emphasis on the management of the impression one is making rather than meaningful contribution

- Lack of innovative thinking, idea sharing, and thought leadership behaviors and much "tell me what to do and I'll do it" behavior

Contributing Factors

The following leadership behaviors lead to the development of Yes-itis:

- Personal insecurity about the worthiness of what you have to offer

- Fear of failure and instituting overly rigid controls and rigor to avoid it

- Spending the majority of time telling others the right way, and little or no time asking what others think

- Asking others what they think, but only reinforcing thoughts that concur with your own perspective

- Sarcastic or disapproving language when questioned

- Making dismissive comments to people who seem to disagree with you

- Feeling pressure to perform or prove yourself

- Changing behaviors in others by stamping out perceived dissent with positional power

- Sending unapproachable signals to others with your body language

- Rewarding only those who agree with you

- Showing approval and warmth only to those in your inner circle

- Insisting that most decisions go through you for approval

- Entirely changing the work of others and their suggestions to make their proposals reflect your current thinking

Yes-itis is tricky to treat, as it is often a by-product of the Robot Syndrome and "In No One We Trust" Toxicity. Yes-itis creeps into your organization when fear is rampant.

When the ramifications of being honest, presenting an alternate point of view, or suggesting an alternate path forward are deemed permanently career destroying, Yes-itis begins to take root.

Like a ravaging wildfire, the ailment spreads across the organization, and people begin to "yes" you to death and carefully manage the impressions they make in front of you. What's happening behind your back may be different altogether, as Yes-itis usually manifests in front of you, the leader, and subsides when you are not present.

> ## *Main Cause of Yes-itis:*
> Failure to empower others and low tolerance for risk

YES-ITIS
Leadership Remedy & Treatment Plan

Many of us move into leadership roles because we are good at getting things done. We make things happen and work hard to push an agenda forward. We are rewarded for taking charge and executing well. This go-getter, move forward attitude often gets us branded as a "leader."

As a reward for getting results, you are put in charge of more and more people, who in turn can help you make *more* things happen. This is usually the point when you suddenly realize you no longer can do everything yourself or know everything that's going on.

Knowing what to do and telling people how to do it is no longer an effective mechanism for you to get results and move things forward. Fear and panic set in.

After all, you are the one accountable for the results. You are the one entrusted to lead the group to the desired outcome. You are responsible; it's your middle name. That's why you got your job in the first place. If you screw up, they'll think you're incompetent and fire you on the spot. Then you'll be branded a failure . . . you of all people. You don't like the direction this is going one bit.

How will you maintain control?

You revert to doing what you know how to do well and what has worked for you in the past. You tighten control. You make sure you know everything that is going on and that you are the center of the sphere. You tell people what to do and how to do it. You carefully monitor every detail and push forward (at least you think you do). There is no room for discussion or disagreement—you have limited time, energy, and bandwidth.

You see employees who want to discuss alternatives as obstacles to getting done what you need to get done. Your impatience and resolve permeate the organization. Employees decide to stay out of your way. They learn to do what you say and succumb to being merely "resources" to help you do what you plan. The unspoken message to all is that you are in charge, you are all knowing, and you have all the answers. Others are simply there to serve you.

Something's Got To Give

No matter how good you are, you can't be an individual contributor AND lead a large group of people. With a small group, it's doable, but with a large department or organization—eventually something's got to give.

People leadership is not the same as project management. You can take an "I can do it all" approach to run a project, but not an organization full of people.

You can have a vision, a direction, and clear expectations, but being in control of every detail of how that vision gets executed and how people act and think stifles innovation, creativity, and significantly decreases engagement. People begin to act out of fear and compliance rather than feel they are making meaningful contributions. Their brains are essentially turned-off because *your* brain is the only one deemed important.

At some point, you will fail or burnout (or both). You will realize your greatest fear, despite all your efforts not to. You will fail, not due to the incompetence of others, but because you failed to empower your employees, loosen control, tolerate risk, and trust others to find ways to deliver your vision. You will fail because of your inability to lead people instead of project manage them.

If this sounds basic and you are thinking, "I already know this," why then do I see this behavior over and over at the highest echelons of numerous organizations? Why do senior most leaders model Yes-itis behavior even though they know it's a recipe for disaster in the long-term?

Giving up control is risky. If you give up control, you risk failing.

So how do you loosen control and empower others? How do you rid yourself and your organization of Yes-itis?

Ailment #3: Yes-itis

Leadership Remedy:
Empowerment—Loosen the Reins

Treatment Plan:

- Risk
- Results
- Reward

Prognosis:
Advice Following Treatment

Yes-itis Leadership Remedy: *Empowerment—Loosen the Reins*

The *Leadership Remedy* for Yes-itis is Empowerment.

The *Treatment Plan* consists of consists of three components—Risk, Results, and Reward:

Risk

Take the risk of trusting that the competent people on your team will find good, creative solutions and deliver on their commitments. Allow others to try new things and take calculated risks.

Results

Focus on clearly defining the results you want, the parameters around achieving those results, and the accountability you expect. Leave the rest to the capable people who work for you to achieve.

Reward

Encourage creativity, discussion, and problem-solving. Reward people for taking initiative and coming up with innovative solutions.

Ailment #3: Yes-itis

Leadership Remedy:
Empowerment—Loosen the Reins

Treatment Plan:

- Risk
- Results
- Reward

Prognosis:
Advice Following Treatment

"*The dangers of life are infinite, and among them is safety.*" *(Goethe)*

Yes-itis Treatment Plan: *Risk*

Summary

To maximize the contributions of others and to maintain successful results over time, you must risk empowering others to act without your hovering involvement. Learning to let go of control and take this risk is essential to eliminate Yes-itis in your organization and to your long-term success.

Goal

Trust the competent people you hire to deliver results and empower them to do so.

Real World Scenario: Do You Know "Ruth?"

Ruth was considered on the fast track in her organization from the moment she got there. A smart, ambitious, hard-working, and results-oriented engineer, her ability to get things done and her attention to metrics and detail paved her way up to a general management position in a large government contracting company.

In her new role as a general manager overseeing an entire division and line of business, Ruth found herself overwhelmed. Directing and controlling the activities of all the subdivisions and the contracts in play seemed humanly impossible. She had run large programs before, and assumed that a program management approach would work for running a large organization. "How was this any different from a really large program, anyway?" She wondered.

Ruth set out to control the reins of the organization tightly. She implemented rigid and meticulous reporting mechanisms and reviews to ensure she had her finger on the pulse of everything all the time. She insisted that important decisions go through her.

As a result, the organization spent more time creating reports and trying to figure out the answers she wanted than it did creating innovative solutions.

Decisions bottlenecked and actions stalled awaiting Ruth's approval. When Ruth finally did review a proposal, she always changed the work and suggested a different way of handling the situation or approach.

Her team became increasingly frustrated and disempowered, disengaged, and disenchanted. "Just ask her how she wants it done," became the organizational mantra. "Let's not waste time doing and re-doing things. She'll just want it done her way anyway."

The Safety Zone

One of our primary needs as humans is the need for safety. We hold this need in common with most other creatures on the planet. When we take a risk outside our comfort zone, we risk our safety. When we take that risk and have a bad experience, we reinforce our belief that we must stay in our comfort zone to stay safe.

As leaders, the ramifications of taking risks can be great, depending on the risk and the outcome or fallout from a mistake.

In cultures where mistakes are considered permanent failures, Yes-itis is rampant. One mistake can brand you a failure and banish you from positions of leadership forever.

And it matters not whether you personally make the mistake. As leader, you are responsible for the actions and behaviors of everyone in your organization. They make the mistake, and you are the one out. You are the one without a job, trying to find another way to pay that hefty mortgage you acquired as a tax break against the salary and fringe pay you get for being so responsible and for not making mistakes.

Why in the world would you ever risk screwing that scene up?

What may not be evident to you is that you are already taking a big risk. By creating an organization where you control everything and you ask the leaders and bright people you hire to park their brains at the door and let you lead them around on a tight leash, you are setting you and your organization up for failure.

Whether you realize it or not, when you fail to empower others and control everything, you create compliance. Compliance is mere lip service. With sheer compliance, you don't have commitment. Without commitment from the people in your organization, you have a shell of an organization, ready to shatter at the slightest break—and ready to throw you under the bus at the slightest shake-up.

You need people to be invested in your organization. You need the kind of investment that doesn't come from simply getting a paycheck. You need the kind of investment that comes when employees make meaningful contributions and feel as though they are having an impact.

Because You Said So

When your employees park their brains at the door, they've resigned themselves to simply follow your orders, right or wrong. It's the kind of situation ripe for mistakes. Tasks get completed, initiatives begun, and decisions made because "you said so"—not because something makes sense or is the right course of action.

Let's face it. You can't possibly know and understand the context and the players in every part of your organization, so you can't possibly create the best solutions. You need people with active brains who will create the solutions themselves, achieve the goals you jointly put in place, and push back and tell you when something you are thinking makes no sense.

To foster this kind of culture in your organization, you have to take a risk of your own and loosen the reins, and you need to be willing to let others in your organization take calculated risks, too. Mistakes happen. Know it. Accept it. Deal with it. Sure, mistakes can be costly and have great implications—but not taking any risks can have the same affect. It's through our mistakes, we learn. It's through our mistakes, we often achieve our greatest successes.

Treatment Application:
Risk: Questions to Ask Yourself

1. Do you trust the people who work for you to do their jobs well?

2. Have you hired staff who are good at what they do?

3. Have you clearly communicated your expectations?

4. Do you allow people the freedom and creativity to figure out the best ways to execute on your expectations?

5. Are you expecting people to make decisions or do you want them to rely on you for decisions?

6. Do you feel that if you make a mistake, it will be fatal to your career?

7. Do you help others learn and move on from temporary setbacks or failures?

8. Are you the funnel everything related to your organization must go through?

9. Do you believe that you know best and that your way of doing things is the best way to do them?

Treatment Application:
Examples of Risk-Taking Behaviors

Behaviors That Reinforce Low Risk-Taking	Behaviors That Promote Risk-Taking
Not addressing performance gaps or issues	Clear articulation of and upholding high standards of performance
Hiring people who depend on you to do all the thinking	Selecting competent staff members who can deliver on results without excessive guidance
Over-involvement in the details of the jobs of others	Allowing people the freedom to decide upon and handle the details of execution
Weighing in on every decision	Trusting good people to make sound decisions
Magnifying mistakes as fatal	Helping people learn from prudent mistakes and correct them
Reacting to every situation with a "sky is falling," crisis-inducing demeanor	Staying calm and collected while choosing actions
Doing the jobs of others for them	Empowering others to do their jobs

Ailment #3: Yes-itis

Leadership Remedy:
Empowerment—Loosen the Reins

Treatment Plan:

- Risk
- Results
- Reward

Prognosis:
Advice Following Treatment

"If you want to build a ship, don't herd people together to collect wood and don't assign them tasks and work, but rather teach them to long for the endless immensity of the sea."
(Antoine de Saint-Exupery)

Yes-itis Treatment Plan: *Results*

Summary

Focus on clearly defining the results you want, the parameters around achieving that result, the accountability you expect, and then get out of the way to allow the capable people you hired to deliver results. Continuously reinforce your expectations and give ample support, guidance, and feedback as needed along the way.

Goal

Focus on clearly defining the results you want, the parameters around achieving those results, and the accountability you expect.

Real-World Scenario: Do You Know "Kevin?"

Kevin started a small Web design company that in four years grew from a home-based office with two employees to a firm numbering more than 800 in three large cities. As the company grew, Kevin realized quickly that he could not remain involved in every detail and decision as he had been in the early phases of startup. He needed a plan.

Critical to his growth strategy was hiring the right people for his expanding company—people who shared his overarching vision and values around what was important and what he wanted to create, people he could trust to realize his vision without his day-to-day involvement and supervision.

As the company grew and grew, Kevin found himself continuously painting a picture for his new team of what they were there to do, what the company stood for, and what he wanted their products to look like. He made a point to be clear about the results he desired and his expectations for each employee. After all, he really had no choice. The task of steering the organization was monumental. He could not do all the work alone. Only a fool would make such an attempt, and Kevin was no fool. Eventually, all he could do was stand back and let his people do their thing, comfortable that he had done his best to assemble a skilled team.

Now, four years later, his phenomenal success story speaks for itself.

In People We Trust

Trusting others to deliver the results you want requires three key ingredients:

1. You must have the right people in place. There is no substitute for quality.

2. You must be willing to take a leap of faith that the team you have assembled is the right one for the job.

3. You need to make sure employees clearly understand the results you expect, the outcomes you desire, and what the vision of the future looks like and how they'll know when they've achieved it.

Now, "vision" is a mushy word that is often overused. It sometimes connotes a far off, unattainable state that doesn't always seem related to a company's need for more immediate results. I tend to think of vision as simply a picture of the long-term results you desire or you believe are possible for your organization.

I try not to use the word "vision" very much. Why? Because visions evolve and change constantly and are not necessarily fixed. Instead, what I want is something that's more tangible, more concrete, more useful. What I'm after are answers to these questions:

- What results are you looking for, both short-term and long-term, and what direction are you headed in and why?

- What factors are driving the direction?

- What possibilities do you see now?

- What other possibilities can be explored in this direction?

- How can others help shape the future?

- What behaviors are expected as you move in this direction?

- What values must your entire organization uphold in the achievement of the results you are after?

Defining the results you want and your expectations is critical for your organization. So is taking the leap of faith to allow your employees the flexibility and independence they need to achieve their own visions of what is possible.

This premise, when put into action, is a potent remedy for the pervasive condition of Yes-itis that plagues far too many organizations.

If you're thinking, "I already know this. I'm a seasoned leader and have been leading people for a long time," remember that what is common knowledge is not necessarily common practice.

The only way to make something common practice is to notice it, acknowledge it, and then apply it consistently.

Just because we know something doesn't mean we apply it. If that were the case, we wouldn't have a multi-billion dollar diet industry. People already know how to lose weight. Have you seen a diet book that isn't basic?

The question is—how many people apply what they know?

Treatment Application:
Results: Questions to Ask Yourself

1. Do you clearly let people know the direction you are headed and what their roles are?

2. If you are unsure about the direction, do you tell people you are unsure and then ask them to help create and define it?

3. Do you already have a result in your mind but wait for people to keep guessing what it is?

4. Are you open to changing direction?

5. Do you let people know what is negotiable and what is not?

6. Are you clear about who is responsible for what?

7. Do you encourage innovation and creativity in the way results are achieved?

8. Do you have a pre-defined notion of how to achieve these results? If yes, is there a good reason for using that approach and not another?

9. Are you communicating the context to people so that they understand why they are headed in a particular direction?

10. Do you welcome ideas to improve and challenges to the direction you have defined?

Treatment Application:
Tips for Empowering Others to Deliver Results

1. Hire people who are professional, competent, have expertise, and that you have faith in.

2. Clearly tell these competent people the outcomes you desire and set the direction.

3. Let these competent people use their expertise and deliver, refining the outcome with your regular feedback along the way.

4. Don't expect the outcome to be designed and delivered 100% "your way," unless you have a preconceived notion of its design and execution. (If you do—then perhaps you need to hire administrators rather than professionals.)

5. Listen carefully to the rationale and advice from the people you have hired who have expertise in a particular area, rather than thinking you know best.

6. When expectations change, evolve, or shift direction, communicate the changes immediately.

7. Listen, listen, and listen some more.

8. Keep your fingers on the pulse of the execution by getting regular updates along the way.

9. Offer reinforcement and guidance and remind your team of the importance of what they are doing.

Ailment #3: Yes-itis

Leadership Remedy:
Empowerment—Loosen the Reins

Treatment Plan:

- Risk
- Results
- **Reward**

Prognosis:
Advice Following Treatment

"In the arena of human life the honors and rewards fall to those who show their good qualities in action." (Aristotle)

Yes-itis Treatment Plan: *Reward*

Summary

How you reward behavior and the messages you send with those rewards is critical to ridding your organization of Yes-itis. Reward initiative, honesty, risk-taking, commitment, teamwork, and courage, rather than compliant behavior.

Goal

Encourage creativity, discussion, and problem-solving and reward people for taking initiative and coming up with innovative solutions.

Real World Scenario: Do You Know "Helen?"

Helen sees herself as a leader who believes in rewarding the people who work for her.

One year, when it was time for annual merit pay increases, she was the loudest voice lobbying Human Resources about her team. "They work so hard," she advocated. "They always stay late and work on weekends to get the work done."

Helen was shocked when feedback from an employee engagement survey revealed low scores on rewards and recognition, despite her efforts. She felt betrayed and insulted. She believed the reason for the poor feedback was the company's inability to provide her team with higher increases. She figured her employees felt disrespected by the percentages she was able to offer. "A 1 or 2% raise is insulting to their efforts," she explained.

Send In the Reinforcements

When we attempt to change or reinforce behavior, we reward those behaviors we desire. Doing so tells the recipient that we appreciate and like the behavior, and that it aligns with our expectations. Reward also increases the chances that her or she will continue to exhibit the behavior.

Humans respond to reward and punishment. We survey our environments and quickly discern which behaviors will reap favor and reward and which will garner punishment. If we fear being ostracized or banished, we weigh those consequences. More often than not, if we feel the need to keep our employment and don't have the fortitude or privilege to look for or find employment elsewhere, we comply with the behavior that receives the reward of staying employed, at least temporarily.

When you are attempting to rid your organization of Yes-itis, how you reward behavior and the messages you send with those rewards becomes paramount. If you acknowledge and reward those who operate in a minion-like fashion and "yes" you to death, then everyone around you will pick up on that cue. Rewards will be seen as a result of "kissing the ring" or bowing to the emperor, and employees will do what they need to maintain their safety and mimic the behavior you are reinforcing.

A clear way to rid your organization of Yes-itis is to reward initiative, honesty, risk-taking, commitment, teamwork, and courage, rather than compliant behavior.

It's really pretty simple. Are you rewarding these things so that you reinforce the behaviors you are looking for and negate a Yes-itis culture? If not, what do you need to do change?

Treatment Application:
Reward: Questions to Ask Yourself

1. Do you encourage people to offer ideas, suggestions, or come up with new ways of doing things?

2. When people disagree with you or your approach, do you react with acceptance and openness, or with disapproval and banishment?

3. Do you include everyone or only those who are your "advocates"?

4. Would people on your team say you have an inner circle of "chosen employees"?

5. Do you get visibly upset or irritated when people don't agree with you?

6. Do you regularly acknowledge the successes and contributions of others?

7. Do you show others how much you value their contributions, competence, and ideas, as well as how much you value them as unique human beings on your team?

8. Do you shun those who offer contrary perspectives?

9. Do you tell more than you ask?

10. Do you listen?

11. Do you listen to find holes in an argument or to learn?

Treatment Application:
Examples of Behaviors that Reinforce & Squash Initiative

REINFORCE	SQUASH
Asking for and listening to ideas, advice, opinions, and expertise	Thinking you know best and ignoring internal expertise or ideas
Giving credit to others for their ideas and work	Taking all the credit for ideas and work
Seeing a challenging thought or idea as a valuable perspective	Visibly disapproving of any differing perspectives
Seeking different perspectives	Shunning those with perspectives other than your own
Admitting that you don't have all the answers	Acting as if you have all the right answers
Complimenting others on their ideas	Failing to acknowledge others for their ideas
Publicly acknowledging the contributions of others	Ignoring the contributions of others
Celebrating success	Letting others feel that their success is just part of the job expectation
Helping people see the larger impact of their accomplishments and contributions	Highlighting flaws and challenges only
Telling others that you value and appreciate them	Having a "what have you done for me lately?" attitude
Showing others that you care about them and their continued development	Seeing people as expendable, merely "human resources" to achieve a business outcome

Ailment #3: Yes-itis

Leadership Remedy:
Empowerment—Loosen the Reins

Treatment Plan:

* Risk
* Results
* Reward

Prognosis:
Advice Following Treatment

Yes-itis Prognosis: *Advice Following Treatment*

Yes-itis may seem innocuous to you as a leader, and may be difficult to detect.

Why?

Because we all love to be adored and want to assume that people agree with us and support us because we are brilliant, wonderful, or fabulous leaders.

While all of these glowing descriptors may be true, they may not be the reasons people in organizations dote over you and agree with and implement without question everything you say. Instead, the people in your organization may be under the grip of Yes-itis, and changing your behavior as a leader is the remedy.

Empowering others by loosening the reigns of your control is the key to exterminating this ailment. Taking the risk of allowing others to take risks, clearly communicating the results you desire, letting others figure out how to achieve those results, and rewarding people for their risk-taking, innovation, courage, and commitment is the way to eliminate Yes-itis.

You may experience extreme discomfort while doing this, and perhaps even a hefty dose of self-doubt, insecurity, and fear. After all, holding the reins tightly may be comfortable and secure for you. You may wonder about your own contributions, especially if you no longer control everything that happens in your organization.

Over time, you will get more comfortable and set the right amount of checks and balances in place so that you are informed and can chart and lead the course, but not have to supervise the drive of all the ships to harbor.

People in your organization will feel more empowered and less afraid to tell you their opinions, or when the boat is off course. The yeses you will get then will be genuine expressions of confidence and commitment.

Ailment #4: Blame Disorder

Make No Mistake About It

From the time we were toddlers, people have told us not to make mistakes or do something wrong, admonishing us with unfavorable messages such as "Bad girl!" or "Bad boy!" or words as guilt inducing as "I am so disappointed in you."

When we were asked, "Who did that?" in reaction to something we did or said that was deemed unfavorable, our response of accountability, "I did," usually yielded some sort of punishment or consequence. Of course, the punishment was meant to incentivize us not to do it again.

The simple act of being accountable and taking ownership for our mistake reinforced our honesty, and being honest often overrode the temporary failing of the mistake we made.

As long as we felt safe and loved, the temporary failing and punishment did not jeopardize our emotional safety to any large degree, and the punishment was not indicative of our value as a person. We could separate the fact that just because our actions were mistakes did not constitute that we, as people, were "failures" or were "bad." The mistakes were not terminal, we were not banished, and we were usually rewarded—often much to our surprise—for being honest and accountable.

In many organizations, the consequences of making a mistake threaten our fundamental safety needs as humans. In environments of low trust, plagued with "In No One We Trust" Toxicity and coupled with the Robot Syndrome and Yes-itis, making a mistake or risking failure is deemed a big threat to our safety. In our minds, we feel disposable, as though no one in the organization truly cares about our well-being—we could be ostracized, fired, or banished from the kingdom!

Fear permeates our minds and we adopt and exhibit behaviors that protect us from failure, or better yet, the semblance of failure.

When we make mistakes or fail at something, which we all do, we become fearful that the consequence of our failure will be exaggerated and that our worth as an employee or follower will be denigrated and irreparable.

Under these conditions, the ailment of Blame Disorder is sure to manifest and thrive. Low trust, fear, lack of human connection and authenticity, and low empowerment are ripe soil for a culture of low accountability and covering up or blaming others for mistakes.

What is Blame Disorder?

Blame Disorder is an organizational ailment that manifests as a result of low accountability for mistakes and results due to fear of repercussions from failure. Blame Disorder is often modeled, reinforced, and/or instigated by the leader and mimicked by the rest of the organization.

Common Symptoms

- Lack of a systems mentality and a compartmentalized, department-focused way of looking at responsibility

- Assigning blame to others in the system when something fails

- Failure to assume responsibility for problems

- Rationalizing that problems are out of one's sphere of control

- Assigning accountability for issues to others with a "that's not my problem" attitude

Contributing Factors

The following conditions contribute to the development of leadership behaviors that lead to chronic Blame Disorder:

- Lack of human connection

- Low trust environment

- Low tolerance for risk

- Lack of empowerment

- Fear

- Inability to see things as part of a larger system

- Disengagement

- Over-competitiveness and personal posturing for position

- Internal organizational politics

> ### *Main Cause of Blame Disorder:*
> Fear of Failure

BLAME DISORDER
Leadership Remedy & Treatment Plan

The treatment of Blame Disorder is tricky because it manifests as a result of the Robot Syndrome, "In No One We Trust" Toxicity, and Yes-itis. If those ailments are not cured first, Blame Disorder cannot be treated or eradicated. If the other ailments *have* been addressed, then a thorough leadership remedy and treatment regimen is recommended.

For many people who are used to competing, succeeding, achieving, and winning, making a mistake or experiencing failure is hard to swallow.

In modern Western society, self-worth is often enmeshed with achievement. The more we achieve and succeed, the more worthy we feel and the more worthy we appear to others. This dynamic becomes second nature, and we begin to derive our self-images as synonymous with our titles, the status these titles imply to others, our accumulation of material objects, and our achievements.

Achievement and success become part of our worth as person. To fail means that we are less worthy to ourselves, and the story we tell ourselves is that we are less worthy to others, or that we are NGE (Not Good Enough).

Take this kind of personal propensity and couple it with organizational dynamics of low trust, fear, lack of empowerment and safety, and a low tolerance for mistakes and failure, and even the slightest of mistakes becomes seemingly fatal.

Most of us are convinced that being exiled from the kingdom, or organization, is sure to happen as a result of failure. Or, equally as bad, we envision ourselves exiled to a job that is "beneath" us or is clearly prescribed for those who have not quite measured up.

In order to expel this deadly disorder from our organizations, as leaders we must first set an example and model different types of behavior.

You must first be persistent, patient, and vigilant in your quest to stamp out the infectious Robot Syndrome, "In No One We Trust" Toxicity, and Yes-itis manifestations. Then, and only then, can you start to address and wipe out the resulting condition of Blame Disorder. To do so, you must begin to model behaviors of accountability and expect this same accountability from everyone in your organization . . . and it starts with you.

Ailment #4: Blame Disorder

Leadership Remedy:
Accountability—Expect and Own Mistakes

Treatment Plan:

- Acknowledgement
- Awareness
- Advancement

Prognosis:
Advice Following Treatment

Blame Disorder Leadership Remedy: *Accountability—Expect and Own Mistakes*

The *Leadership Remedy* for Blame Disorder is Accountability.

The *Treatment Plan* consists of three components—Acknowledgement, Awareness, and Advancement:

Acknowledgement

Admit when you have made a mistake, had an error in judgment, or created an unintended outcome, and take full responsibility for the subsequent result. This includes not blaming others as the source of your mistake or cause of your actions.

Awareness

Step back and see yourself in an imaginary mirror as an independent object inside the mirror. Objectively assess your behavior, intent, and thinking in your decisions and actions.

Advancement

Learn from and move forward from setbacks with courage, confidence, and experience.

Ailment #4: Blame Disorder

Leadership Remedy:
Accountability—Expect and Own
Mistakes

Treatment Plan:

- Acknowledgement
- Awareness
- Advancement

Prognosis:
Advice Following Treatment

*"It is common sense to take a method and try it.
If it fails, admit it frankly and try another. But
above all, try something."*
(Franklin D. Roosevelt)

Blame Disorder Treatment Plan:
Acknowledgement

Summary

The first step in creating accountability and eradicating Blame Disorder in your organization is to model acknowledgment by accepting full blame for mistakes and admitting your failures instead of pointing fingers. This provides a strong example of accountability.

Goal

Admit your mistakes rather than try to cover them up or blame others.

Real-World Scenario: Do You Know "Vanessa?"

A major retail bank was in a downward spiral, losing much of its market share to a new bank cropping up in the region. This competitor had a creative marketing approach and was bombarding the general public with a series of clever television advertisements that emphasized their less than traditional approach to marketing.

Vanessa, the retail bank's Vice President of Marketing, had taken a hard stance on the bank's marketing approach several years ago when they were trying to re-position themselves after a host of bank failures. She had worked with an ad agency to position the bank as a steady and traditional presence in the community. "People want stability from their banks," she advised the rest of the executive team.

But as new players began to enter the market, Vanessa's staff began to question the long-term viability of their traditional approach. "Perhaps we can start to blend our marketing messages to reflect a more contemporary attitude," some suggested. Her colleagues also began to question her approach. "Your advertising is killing us. We are out of touch with the consumer!"

Her reaction to the perceived criticism was to defend her actions. "How could I possibly take a new and different approach when this team is so conservative? No one here is ever willing to back something new, and the age-old excuse is that we are a conservative and stable bank. I give you what you want, and when it doesn't work the way you want it, you attack me and my approach."

Risky Business

Acknowledging one's own misperceptions, mistakes, or miscalculations is difficult. When we make decisions, there is always an element of risk involved.

Where to live, who to marry, what job to take, what direction to take, how much education to get, what car to buy—these are all decisions that have impact and consequences, some of which could shape the course of our lives.

After we make and execute a decision, we can find out that we made a mistake from a variety of indicators. Even if we acted in a relatively prudent manner, our choices do not always garner the results we want or expect for numerous reasons.

We learn from these errors in judgment, and we try to evaluate lessons learned for the next decision. We learn to be prudent, but not so prudent as to be paralyzed. We can never have enough information to make a decision that eliminates all risk.

The important thing we learn is to take the information we have at the time, consider the risks, ask for various perspectives, and then make a choice and act.

Inaction, as we know, is often the result of fear of making a mistake, and the propensity to become paralyzed by that fear.

As leaders in an organization, the complexity of the decisions we face increases dramatically. There are so many unknown factors, circumstances, and influences on the outcomes of our decisions. When combined with continuous change, varying perspective, and the absence of facts, the element of risk increases exponentially, as does the potential of a perceived "mistake."

Being able to model action and decision-making under these circumstances is an essential part of being a leader. So is realizing that you, and those around you, will not always get it right and that there isn't always a clear-cut "right" answer.

If you want to eradicate Blame Disorder from your organization, you must be able to acknowledge when a decision you make or an action you take is a mistake or its consequence is not what you anticipate or expect . . . and be able to move on.

We all have reasons why we do things and can rationalize all the causes of our behavior. But in the end—the buck stops with us. When we point the finger of blame at others, we lose credibility and destroy accountability.

As a leader, you must be willing to own the decisions you make, the consequences of them, and make new decisions to correct any unanticipated results. Acknowledging your mistakes or perceived failures is the critical first step to modeling accountability.

Think back to our discussion of the Robot Syndrome and how it relates to your sense of self. If you are coming from a place of insecurity, fear, and reactivity and you are not grounded in a solid sense of self, your tendency will be to protect and control.

Part of protecting yourself is blaming others and rationalizing why you did something, rather than owning the result of your actions. Your security with yourself influences how you react to a failure or mistake. That is why the treatment for Robot Disorder and becoming grounded in your own presence and sense of self is so important—it has a ripple effect to all of other ailments described in this book.

Treatment Application:
Acknowledgement: Questions to Ask Yourself

- Do you recognize you are not infallible and will make mistakes?

- Do you understand that certainty about anything does not exist?

- Do you realize that you are not all knowing and will not always be "right?"

- Do you see that you have inherent biases when making decisions?

- If the consequences of making a mistake seem intolerable to you, do you find ways to rationalize your actions instead of acknowledging their impact?

- Do you resent others when you fail at something?

- Do you look for someone to blame or "extinguish" when something goes wrong?

- Do you model accountability by owning an error in judgment without the need to "hang" others for the impact?

Treatment Application:

Comparing Accountable Behaviors and Blaming Behaviors

ACCOUNTABLE BEHAVIORS	BLAMING BEHAVIORS
Admitting an error	Making excuses for why an error occurred
Reviewing lessons learned from a mistake or failure	Finding a "fall guy" to fire after a mistake is made
Expecting mistakes and learning from them	Expecting perfection 100% of the time
Asking others for feedback	Only telling others what they did wrong
Assessing impact and taking corrective action	Spending your time searching for a "fall guy"
Asking for help to bounce back from a mistake	Letting others know how they caused the mistake
Creating a mitigation plan and executing it quickly	Staying stuck in your position
Admitting your biases	Pointing out the biases of others

Ailment #4: Blame Disorder

Leadership Remedy:
Accountability—Expect and Own
Mistakes

Treatment Plan:

- Acknowledgement
- Awareness
- Advancement

Prognosis:
Advice Following Treatment

*"To make no mistakes is not in the power of man;
but from their errors and mistakes the wise and
good learn wisdom for the future."*
(Plutarch)

Blame Disorder Treatment Plan: *Awareness*

Summary

A big part of increasing accountability is the ability to step back and see yourself as an independent object inside a mirror. Objectively looking from the outside in and assessing the behavior, intent, and thinking involved in your decisions and actions allows you to see yourself as a player in a story. This enables you to see your role in the outcome of the story and to choose different actions.

Goal

Step back and watch yourself as though you were in a movie and objectively analyze the behaviors you see.

Real World Scenario: Do You Know "Mark?"

Mark is an entrepreneur. He founded three different companies in the past decade. The first two companies were full of starts and stops—bursts of enthusiasm and energy followed by lulls of inaction and lack of follow-through. Mark's biggest supporters advised him to get someone to help with operations and business development, as his downfall seemed to come from lack of attention to those important areas.

Mark was excited about his products, services, and the potential ways he could help his customers, but not at all about the nitty-gritty details of starting and building a business. He assumed that his talent and brilliance alone in the area of branding would be enough to attract customers. After all, he was the branding master and could help anyone! Much to his surprise, his first two businesses showed lackluster results and he had to cease investment.

His latest venture, a branding company for entrepreneurs and small businesses, has taken off beyond his wildest expectations.

What was different this time around?

Mark hired three new people to help him, apparently learning from his previous mistakes. He also admits that his ego was a big factor in the failure of his first venture.

"I thought I was invincible and wouldn't listen to anyone," he recalls. "I just couldn't look at myself and what I was doing objectively. I couldn't look at myself realistically in the mirror. If there is one thing I have learned, is that you have to be able to look at yourself and self-correct."

The Man in the Mirror

In order to learn from experience and increase internal decision-making capacity, we must learn to observe ourselves. Have you ever seen a movie where the protagonist dies, separates from his or her body, and then looks down from above, as though watching a movie?

The ability to "observe" yourself is much like that. It is the ability to take a piece of your mind and separate it from your body and behaviors, becoming an objective observer of yourself. It requires you to put your ego away and look at yourself from the outside, as if looking at someone else in a mirror.

Michael Jackson's song, "The Man in the Mirror," describes this perfectly.

Holding a mirror up to ourselves and seeing ourselves as we really are is difficult to do, since we are so attached to our own concept of self and self-image. If we are to rid ourselves and our organizations of Blame Disorder, the ability to do this regularly needs to become a common practice.

Part of exterminating Blame Disorder is becoming personally accountable for our choices, actions, and behaviors, in spite of the risks of doing so. Many times, the risk is merely that we look in the mirror and can't bear what we see, so we delude ourselves and don't look—yet flash the mirror at everyone else.

Being able to acknowledge your mistakes and flaws, and then reflect on what you have learned from your experience so you can think about ways to adjust your future behavior is a big part of self-awareness and the ability to adjust your actions.

The realization that you are in control of your own behavior, can learn from each experience and each choice you make, and can adjust your choices in the future as you assimilate your learning is an integral part of personal growth.

When we stay defensive, reactive, and protective in a blaming posture, we stay stunted and stuck. Moving forward requires deep awareness through self-reflection, self-analysis, and assimilation of what we have learned to allow us to choose future behavior.

Blame Disorder cannot be eradicated without this process of personal accountability from you as the leader.

Separating from your ego and looking at yourself as a player in a movie is a good way to practice doing this. Can you objectively see your actions and motivations without being attached to them from this angle of observation?

Treatment Application:
Awareness: Questions to Ask Yourself

- Do you regularly rise up to the mountain view of a situation and observe the action happening in the valley, including yourself, from that vantage point?

- Can you separate yourself from the situation you are in and look at yourself as one of the players/contributors to the unfolding events?

- When you are uncomfortable with something you did or are doing, do you adjust your behavior and learn from it?

- Do you feel the need to be perfect and constantly achieving in order to feel validated?

- Do you consider the impact of your behavior on others and on the outcomes of situations?

- Do you admit when you are wrong and apologize to others if your actions cause unintended consequences?

- Are you confident enough to realize that most setbacks and failures are part of moments in a time continuum and are not permanent?

- Are your intentions pure and ethical?

Treatment Application:
3 Tips to Increase Self-Reflection and Awareness

1. **Spend 5 minutes at the end of each day reviewing your actions and feelings.**

   Recall the day's events and your behaviors throughout the day as a movie. Observe yourself as an actor in this movie. Notice what you learn about yourself, your feelings, and the motivations of your actions. Notice the story you are telling yourself about the day's events and your role in them. Ask yourself if you like the story you see and think about ways you can change the story tomorrow if you don't.

2. **Take a 30-minute lunch break by yourself at least twice per week.**

   Don't look at your email, read the paper, or make phone calls. Just sit quietly and eat your lunch. Tune in to what you are feeling that day and what your energy is like. Think about your interactions so far in the day. Ask yourself if you are being the person you want to be today.

3. **Practice Freeze Framing.**

   During an interaction with someone, try "freeze framing." Look at the person's body language, face, gestures, and listen carefully to the tone of the interaction. Watch and listen closely and try to determine the feeling tone underneath the interaction. When you pause occasionally and tune into the other person rather than just yourself and your message, your awareness increases and things you didn't even notice can come to light.

Ailment #4: Blame Disorder

Leadership Remedy:
Accountability—Expect and Own
Mistakes

Treatment Plan:

- Acknowledgement
- Awareness
- **Advancement**

Prognosis:
Advice Following Treatment

*"Success seems to be connected with action.
Successful people keep moving. They make
mistakes, but they don't quit."
(Conrad Hilton)*

Blame Disorder Treatment Plan:
Advancement

Summary

In organizations, leaders paralyzed by fear perpetuate Blame Disorder, as they are afraid of being ousted. This fear is also the enemy of resilience, learning, growth, and moving forward. Practicing acknowledgement of an error or of difficult feedback, objective self-reflection in order to assimilate and learn from the experience, and advancing forward are the key practices needed to combat Blame Disorder.

Goal

To learn from and move forward from setbacks with courage, confidence, and experience.

Real-World Scenario: Do You Know "Len?"

Len was a client I had several years ago who was up for a key Vice President position. He was smart, personable, well-liked by his direct reports, and certainly one of the best in his field. He certainly seemed the obvious choice for the job. When his seemingly less qualified or spectacular colleague was selected for the job instead, Len was stunned. He was even more stunned at the explanation he received from the president doing the hiring.

"You intimidate your peers with your pushing," he was told. "You are so forward-looking and innovative that you can appear out of touch with the culture here. We needed someone a bit more grounded and able to speak the language to meet people where they are to push them forward gradually."

This feedback struck Len to the core. It made no sense to him and he was convinced the president was crazy and out to get him.

"They are envious that I am smarter than they are," he reasoned.

After a few months, Len had time to step outside himself and look at the organization and the system with himself as a player in it. He realized that to influence this particular system, he had to slow down and let people catch up. He needed to modulate his push forward, so that others could digest what he already knew. He let go of blame and bitterness, and de-personalized the feedback. He adjusted his behavior and was promoted a year later.

A Vicious Cycle

When we have made a mistake or taken a risk that didn't pan out the way we wanted, we can become overly cautious about acting or taking such a risk again.

But being truly accountable and ridding yourself and your organization of Blame Disorder requires a great amount of personal resilience. Like Frank Sinatra sings, you must "pick yourself up, brush yourself off, and start all over again."

It is easy for us to get caught up in insecurity or even self-pity when we have an experience that doesn't go the way we like. To take it even further, when we have to publicly acknowledge or accept our own roles in what has happened, we may tell ourselves that we will never put ourselves in that situation or position again. Paralysis seeps in and we err on the side of inaction, which can become a vicious cycle.

The very cause of Blame Disorder is what needs to be overcome in order to rid ourselves of the ailment, and that's "fear"—fear of failure, fear of being outcast, fear of being ousted, fear of losing, and fear of being deemed unworthy.

Moving forward takes courage, confidence, and a positive mindset.

Advancement from setbacks models leadership and sets the tone for the entire organization. What behaviors are you modeling? Is your organization one that encourages calculated risks, learns from setbacks, and moves forward; or is it one that blames others and gets stuck in its own self-perpetuating fear?

Treatment Application:
Advancement: Questions to Ask Yourself

1. What learning do you glean from a setback?

2. How do seeming failures enhance your successes?

3. What is the absolute best outcome you can create?

4. What keeps you from trying?

5. What happens if you don't try?

6. What do want to change about your response to setbacks?

7. Do you support or sabotage your own efforts?

8. How does a setback experience improve your future attempts?

9. What else do you need to learn?

10. Who are you becoming?

Treatment Application:
10 Tips to Keep Moving Forward

1. Realize that everything you tell yourself is a story you have created to explain or rationalize something from your perspective.

2. You can always change the perspective and the story.

3. Don't be attached to the outcome. Things change and evolve.

4. Don't take yourself too seriously. Unless it can kill you, it isn't fatal.

5. Recognize that you are human just like everyone else, even if you find that hard to accept at times.

6. Remind yourself of your past successes.

7. Every experience you have can serve to teach you something. Look for the learning.

8. Apply what you learn and keep expecting to learn more.

9. Stay grounded, confident, and humble.

10. Refuse to accept defeat or failure as a permanent state.

Ailment #4: Blame Disorder

Leadership Remedy:
Accountability—Expect and Own Mistakes

Treatment Plan:

- Acknowledgement
- Awareness
- Advancement

Prognosis:
Advice Following Treatment

Blame Disorder Prognosis: *Advice Following Treatment*

Treating Blame Disorder in your organization starts with you. Just like the other organizational ailments, your leadership behaviors set the tone for the culture while your actions model the behaviors for others to follow. If you are plagued with low accountability in your organization, you must be diligent about modeling the behaviors associated with the treatment plan.

- Do you expect mistakes and setbacks and *acknowledge* them or do you point fingers and look for scapegoats?

- Do you regularly exhibit an ability to self-reflect and look at yourself and your actions objectively and course correct from this place of objective *awareness?*

- Do you model continued *advancement* in spite of setbacks and keep moving forward resiliently by learning from your experience?

Your ability to do these things will go a long way in the eradication of Blame Disorder in your organization. When you hold yourself accountable in this way and provide an environment of learning and resilience to both yourself and the competent people you hired, then Blame Disorder is sure to disappear.

Be careful, though. Like all the other ailments we have discussed, Blame Disorder treatment is fragile and cannot be simply applied and then stopped. Curing Blame Disorder takes consistent work, attention, and continuous treatment. You cannot get lazy and forget to apply the treatment plan, or the disorder will take over again.

Ailment #5: Energy Breakdown

Drains and Gains

When you walk into a room and really pay close attention to the unspoken undertones, can you feel the energy of the group? Can you sense whether the tone is serious or upbeat, and whether the energy of the group is high or low? Most of us can without speaking a word. Energy is palpable, and we can feel it without really explaining or understanding how.

Energy has a charge, and the charge is contagious. Ever play an upbeat song and suddenly the mood of everyone in the room transforms from neutral to happy—and maybe even singing along? Now that's energy.

We know that everything in us and around us is energy. It only makes sense that this energy is a type of charge that can be either positive or negative or low or high, much like a battery. We are all made of energy, and just like a battery, we need recharging. We need time to replenish and "fill up" so we can operate at full capacity. Not only do we need to recharge, but we also need to be surrounded by an energy field that promotes the kind of charge we want to exude.

If we are surrounded by a negatively charged environment, then our charge will vibrate negative. Negative begets negative. Positive begets positive.

Paying attention to energy is critical in organizations.

Is the energy charge in your organization predominantly negative or positive? Is there time allotted for people to replenish and recharge their energy so the quality of what is being produced is what counts, and not merely the quantity?

What I observe in organizations is that we pay very little attention to the type and the quality of the energy everyone brings to the table. We require more and more discretionary effort, and expect leaders and employees to be "on" almost 24 x 7.

While on one hand, it sounds like a good plan—because we can hire less people to do the same amount of work—it's actually a really bad idea. What we have created is a chronic ailment that permeates organizations, a chronic ailment that is difficult to spot on the surface unless we pay close attention.

Running on Empty

Stress, fatigue, weight gain, high blood pressure, cholesterol issues, lack of sleep, poor nutritional and exercise habits, a general feeling of ennui, and lack of vitality embody many of the leaders in our organizations. A subdued, deadened sense of enthusiasm and passion becomes the ordinary way of operating—it becomes "normal" and the expected.

We gain a false sense of increased productivity and this way of working and living becomes part of what we expect as the price we pay for the lives we live and the jobs we have. The low energy level permeates the organization, and we keep running on empty, with a propensity to stay in a negative charge.

We focus on continuously "doing," rather than pausing to consider who and what we are "being" in the process. The "doing" takes center stage, and the more we "do," the more we think we have accomplished. No wonder this ailment has spread like a virus to epidemic proportions in our organizations and lives. We come to think of it as normal and the price of so-called "success."

As a leader, how can you expect your employees to be engaged fully when you are all running on empty and negative? How can you be excited and passionate at work when you are tired and lethargic, and just going to meeting after meeting without a refresh?

How can an organization expect people to be innovative, when they are insulated and so busy going from one thing to the next, that they have no time or space to generate new ideas and think about what they are doing? And who wants to even think about improving something or starting something new when the idea will ultimately create more work and even less energy?

By the very nature of how we work, we perpetuate mediocrity because excellence requires more capacity and energy than we have. Remember, we are already running on empty.

The ailment that is silently eating away at our organizations and feeding the other four ailments is an Energy Breakdown.

Common Symptoms

- Trying to do too much and frequently feeling lethargic, tired, and exhausted

- Multi-tasking and getting many things done yet not being fully "present" during the activities

- Lack of excitement, enjoyment, passion, and full engagement in most activities

- Feeling disengaged and apathetic most of the day

- Negativity, apathy, and ennui are prevalent feelings

- Neglect of physical body through failure to exercise regularly and eat healthy, nutritious foods

- Spending the bulk of time on work activities and feeling out of balance with little time for other areas of life

- Experiencing numerous intermittent health issues such as high blood pressure, high cholesterol, anxiety attacks, chronic neck and shoulder pain, indigestion, and ulcers

Contributing Factors

The following leadership behaviors contribute to Energy Breakdown:

- Cutting resources without making the requisite adjustments to the scope and size of the workload to match the resources needed

- A production mentality where more is considered better

- Valuing the amount someone produces over quality and innovation

- A focus on and reward for doing more

- Over-reactivity to the environment

- Viewing people as expendable resources

- Bias for action

- Failure to consider the human element

- Failure to consider the quality of human energy as a critical resource

> ### *Main Cause of Energy Breakdown:*
>
> Burnout

ENERGY BREAKDOWN
Leadership Remedy and Treatment Plan

The only way to treat Energy Breakdown in an organization is to acknowledge human energy as a critical and essential component of your organization's success.

You must go back to the fundamental premise that not only are you, the leader, a human being with a body full of energy, but so are your employees. Energy can be full and charged with vitality and vigor, or empty and charged with negative toxins and contagious, disease-spreading vibrations.

In order to achieve the type of employee engagement we continuously say we want in organizations, we are going to have to take action to treat Energy Breakdown and hold not only people, but the quality of the human energy of our people, as our greatest asset.

If we could get away with it, most of us would run our cars without gas. Gas is expensive and stopping to fill up is time-consuming. But we know that without gas, we will not get anywhere, and that the car will not move or take us where we want to go.

With people and energy, things are not so simple. We can fill up with foods lacking the nutrients we need and still keep moving, deprive ourselves of adequate sleep yet stay awake with caffeine, and fail to recharge and replenish our energy but still keep going. We can operate like zombies on a permanent artificial charge until something drastic happens and our bodies produce an illness that causes us to stop in our tracks and take notice.

The quality of our energy matters. It is of utmost importance to our organizations and to our lives. The charge we run on can be a source of positivity, creativity, vitality, and passion—but to be so, it must be nourished, maintained, replenished, and honored.

When we "honor" our energy, we realize that the unseen energy we exude as humans is an underlying layer of what gets created in our presence. Maintaining a full tank of positively charged energy as a "field" around us is essential if we want that type of energy to be transferred to the organizations in which we work. You as the leader hold the key to the type of energy that prevails in your organization. By honoring your own energy, you bring an energy field with you that is charged and full of vitality. In kind, you honor the energy of those around you and insist on renewal. You also serve as a magnetic charge—exuding positive charges to the energy field of your organization and sparking a positive contagion to those around you.

Ailment #5: Energy Breakdown

Leadership Remedy:
Balance—Honor Your Energy

Treatment Plan:

- Listen
- Limits
- Laugh

Prognosis:
Advice Following Treatment

Energy Breakdown Leadership Remedy: *Balance—Honor Your Energy*

The *Leadership Remedy* for Energy Breakdown is Balance.

The *Treatment Plan* consists of three components—Listen, Limits, and Laugh.

In order to begin treatment and rid your organization of this ailment, you must first treat yourself and honor your own energy.

Listen

Be attuned to the signals your body sends you and take care of yourself.

Limits

Set boundaries and limits on how much you can take on at one time and set realistic priorities.

Laugh

Lighten up and monitor/control the quality, tone, and charge of your own energy.

Ailment #5: Energy Breakdown

Leadership Remedy: Balance—Honor Your Energy

Treatment Plan:

- Listen
- Limits
- Laugh

Prognosis: Advice Following Treatment

"There is more wisdom in your body than in your deepest philosophies." (Friedrich Nietzsche)

Energy Breakdown Treatment Plan: *Listen*

Summary

The first step in treating Energy Breakdown is for leaders to listen to their own bodies and the messages they send. Listen to the signals of fatigue, apathy, and stress. As leader, you set the example for everyone below you. If you are not honoring your energy and listening to your body—and putting everything else first instead—you are telling everyone else that work is more valuable than anything else, including your health.

Goal

To be attuned to the signals your body sends you and take care of yourself.

Real-World Scenario: Do You Know "Peter?"

Peter runs a government consulting practice for a large management firm. He spends most of his days in endless meetings, either internally with partners or externally with large clients working through contract issues or negotiating business deals.

He feels as though he is constantly putting out fires, and hardly has time to catch his breath before he runs to another competing priority. He is chronically trying to "catch up" with his email, treating his smart phone like an appendage, checking it even when he dashes to the restroom. Feeling overwhelmed is a steady state, and he pops acetaminophen pills all day long to ward off the dull headaches that throb in his temples.

He has given up on his former exercise regimen and gained about 30 pounds in the past two years. He keeps telling his doctor that he will lower his cholesterol and start eating better and exercising, but the reality is that his meals are quick and on the run. During a hectic day a sugary doughnut or muffin appeals to him much more than eating hot oatmeal with fruit.

A recent visit to the emergency room on a Monday afternoon stopped him in his tracks. In the middle of a meeting, he felt as though he was having a heart attack, experiencing severe chest pains and difficulty breathing.

After a myriad of tests, the doctor gave him a sober message: "The good news is this was not a heart attack. It's stress and anxiety. The bad news is that stress and anxiety can cause a heart attack with all the other risk factors you have. Your body is sending you a warning—it's time to listen to it."

Maintenance Plan

To think we need a medical emergency or a close call in order to stop in our tracks and start taking care of ourselves is sad.

Our bodies are precious containers and they wear and tear like any container does. But the neglect, disregard, and/or care and nourishing of our bodies is really up to us. Quite often we keep pushing our bodies until they break down completely or threaten to do so, rather than listen to the signals and provide our bodies with consistent and careful maintenance.

Our bodies contain our energy; they need to be listened to and taken care of as a habit and not as an afterthought. Yet everything else that is urgent to us seems more important and paramount, and we neglect the very thing that enables us to do what we do every day—at least until we have an emergency that makes us stop and take notice.

Otherwise, we assume nothing will ever happen to us. We are invincible, made of "stronger stuff." We tell ourselves amazing stories to rationalize our faulty prioritization and neglect of the most essential and valuable asset we will ever have—our health.

First Step

Energy Breakdown is all too real and prevalent in the organizations with which I work. The first step in treating Energy Breakdown is for leaders to listen to their own bodies and the messages they send.

Listen to the signals of fatigue, apathy, and stress. Listen to the headaches or stiff neck and shoulders. Listen to the heart palpitations or sluggishness or anxiety attacks. Listen to your doctor when he or she tells you to eat foods that are more nutritious and exercise at least three times a week.

Listen and do *something*.

Your health is what you will have or not have long after you leave your current organization. As leader, you set the example for everyone below you. If you are not honoring your energy and listening to your body—and putting everything else first instead—you are telling everyone else that is what you expect from them: *"Work comes above and is more valuable than anything else, including your health."*

As leader, you have the ability to change this paradigm by listening to the signs of Energy Breakdown and helping to restore Balance.

Treatment Application:
Listen: Questions to Ask Yourself

1. Do you get sufficient sleep on a regular basis?

2. Do you drink caffeinated beverages/energy drinks to stay alert and awake?

3. Do you suffer from chronic conditions such as headaches, neck and shoulder stiffness and pain, high blood pressure, high cholesterol, or stomach sensitivity? If yes, do you only pop pills to remedy them or do you also adjust your lifestyle and habits?

4. Do you get regular physicals and other routine check-ups and follow the advice of medical professionals?

5. Is your weight at a normal level and do you eat foods with nutrients to nourish your body, or do you eat mostly fast, processed, or "comfort" foods?

6. Do you exercise regularly or are you always too busy to make time for physical activity?

7. Do you often feel tired or lethargic?

8. Do you feel invigorated and full of vitality most days?

9. Is your attitude and emotional state positive, passionate, and hopeful on most days?

10. Do you focus on the negative aspects of life events, or try to see the positive aspects and/or learning?

Treatment Application:
3 Tips to Listen to and Take Care of Your Body

1. **Pay attention to and act upon the messages you get.** Your body sends you messages of caution all the time. When you feel exhausted, make a point to take the time to rest. If you experience chronic headaches or shoulder pain, take actions to minimize the stress that may be causing them. Take soothing baths twice a week, listen to relaxing music, participate in a yoga class, or just lie down and do nothing for 10 minutes. While these remedies sound obvious, they can work if you use them as interventions.

   As I was writing this section, my computer suddenly shut down. The battery was dead. To remedy the situation, I had to stop what I was doing and plug the power cord back in. In much the same way, you have to listen for and act on the messages you get from your body, preferably *before* you wind up in the hospital with a medical crisis that forces you to shut down for good.

2. **Tune into and adjust the quality of your energy.** Practice "tune-ins" at regular intervals of the day. If you are in a series of meetings or going from one thing to another, take a bathroom break. Stand in the hallway, close your eyes, and take a deep breath. Feel the blood flowing in your body. Are you feeling drained, negative, lifeless? Or are you feeling positive, full of vitality and excitement?

   If the meeting you're in is draining your energy, practice using an imaginary "energy shield." Imagine a shield of light surrounding your entire body; picture it emanating from all around you (really, let go of your judging mind and try this—it works). See yourself as charged with that light energy, literally repelling negativity with its force. Think of what is possible today and remember how happy you are to be alive right now, in this moment . . . then go to the bathroom and go back to your meeting wearing that shield.

3. **Commit to changing one bad habit a month.** You know you need to exercise regularly and eat right, yet you have a thousand excuses for why you don't.

Usually when we have bad habits, we try to change them all at once, which results in an all-or-nothing approach. You either go to the gym for an hour, four times per week, or you don't go at all. You either eliminate all junk food and eat only nutritious foods, or you just eat what you always eat. There is no middle ground.

Pick one small thing you want to change each month and commit to it. For example, if you eat too much fast food, commit to eating fast food only once a week that month. The next month, commit to exercising for 15 minutes every day on the weekend. As these new commitments become habits, you can keep revising them and adding more each month until they become your new way of doing things.

Ailment #5: Energy Breakdown

Leadership Remedy:
Balance—Honor Your Energy

Treatment Plan:

- Listen
- **Limits**
- Laugh

Prognosis:
Advice Following Treatment

*"The difference between stupidity and genius is
that genius has its limits."*
(Albert Einstein)

Energy Breakdown Treatment Plan: *Limits*

Summary

The quality of the energy you bring to what you are doing is more important than the quantity. If you are refreshed, energized, and excited, you tend to be more useful and productive. The only way to protect and replenish energy is to set limits and establish clear priorities.

Goal

To set boundaries and limits on how much you can take on at one time and set realistic priorities.

Real World Scenario: Do You Know "Sandra?"

Sandra runs the training and development function for a large insurance and financial services conglomerate. She takes pride in providing customized training and organizational development services to her internal customers, helping each division design programs suited to their particular business and needs.

The pace of requests and the demands of her job have her operating in a chronic reactive mode, and the "shoot from the hip" leadership style of her boss only exaggerates the tone. She seems to be on call 24x7. She sometimes responds to emails at 1:00 am and fields urgent requests to meet with someone the next day and "roll out" a service for him or her in two. She frequently works 12-hour days, and Sunday is usually her day to catch up on the administrative work she has put off all week.

Sandra is distracted, stressed, and harried. She has no time for herself. In the little time she has away from work, she thinks about what she hasn't been able to do. Her energy is low and she looks pale and tired. Her husband worries about the pace, its effect on her and their family, and pleads with her to set some boundaries.

"You can't keep up like this. You need to set some limits. You and this job are out of control."

Sometimes You Have to Say "No"

A big step in "Honoring Your Energy" is setting limits. To treat Energy Breakdown, not only do you need to listen to your body and its signals, but you need to be able to set limits and tell people when you are at maximum capacity.

In organizations today, with the pressure to do more with less and to be seen as conscientious and capable, we are often afraid to set boundaries and limits. We keep doing more and more to show the emperors in the organization that we are worthy to be there and to be leading.

Setting limits makes us appear weak and not able to keep up; setting limits means we are failing—or so we think. We march on like good soldiers, and the ultimate price we pay is visible to us only years later when health fails, our marriages fall apart, or our kids don't know us.

Setting limits is not only an important part of this treatment plan, it is vital to the ultimate long-term health of our organizations (and ourselves). Honoring human energy is about realizing that energy is finite and needs to be rejuvenated and replenished. Burning the candle to the end of the wick just because we can is never a good idea.

The quality of the energy you bring to what you are doing is more important than the quantity. If you attend a meeting, yet are distracted, tired, and barely listening, the value of your contribution is greatly diminished. If you are refreshed, energized, and excited, then what you bring is much more useful and productive.

The same is true with your employees. Do you want them present regardless of energy level, or do you want them present and engaged?

If the answer is the latter, then you must care about the quality of the energy they (and you) bring to the table, and the only way to protect and replenish energy is to set limits and establish clear priorities among all the competing demands that come our way.

Treatment Application:
Limit: Questions to Ask Yourself

1. Do you have trouble saying "no" to taking on more because you fear you'll appear less competent?

2. Do you deliver on the things you commit to with high quality or do you value quantity over quality?

3. If you did less things better, would it improve the overall quality of what you deliver and your overall competence?

4. What are the real consequences of taking on less as opposed to the story imagined in your mind?

5. What are the real consequences of continuing to operate without clear limits?

6. What are the things right now in your life that you need to say "no" to?

7. What things do you want to make room for and say "yes" to?

8. What adjustments do you need to make?

9. What habits do you need to break?

10. What do you need to start doing differently?

Treatment Application:
4 Tips to Help You Set Limits

1. **Get clear about what's important and what you want to spend time on in all areas of your life. Write it down.**

2. **List things that you are spending time on today and sort them as follows:**

   A = Things that are not that important and should be scrapped

   B = Things that others can do for me

   C = Things that I want to do but don't need to do myself

   D = Things that are clearly important and I want and need to do

   E = Things that I don't want to do

3. **Analyze, evaluate, and shorten your list.**

   • Eliminate things on list "A" completely.

   • Delegate the "B"s

   • Delegate the "C"s

   • Prioritize and space out the "D"s

   • Take a good hard look at the "E"s. Are most of the things you spend time on things that you don't want to do? What does that tell you about your current choices? What new and potentially hard choices do you need to make?

4. **Make some hard decisions and choices about what actions you need to take based on this evaluation and act to set these limits.**

Ailment #5: Energy Breakdown

Leadership Remedy:
Balance—Honor Your Energy

Treatment Plan:

- Listen
- Limits
- Laugh

Prognosis:
Advice Following Treatment

"The most wasted of all days is a day without laughter." (e. e. cummings)

Energy Breakdown Treatment Plan: *Laugh*

Summary

The tone you set as a leader is critical. The tone of your energy is contagious. Positivity and negativity are both tones you can set with your own energy and behavior. If you are serious about treating Energy Breakdown and restoring balance to your organization, you must lighten up and constantly monitor the quality, tone, and charge of your energy. If you don't like what you find, you can make immediate, very simple adjustments.

Goal

To lighten up and monitor the quality, tone, and charge of your own energy.

Real World Scenario: Do You Know "Kurt?"

Kurt works as a controller for a large government agency. His staff consists of accountants and budget analysts that support different divisions within the agency. He knows his numbers well, and has little time for small talk, as he has much to do every day. He carries the weight of the responsibility of his job on his shoulders, and even his stature and demeanor convey a heaviness and serious.

He eats lunch at his desk every day and every conversation with him is "all business" and short. "There is just too much to do," he insists when members of his staff try to engage him in conversation. He seems distracted and checks his smart phone when others talk to him, as if disinterested in the trivial things they are communicating.

"He needs to lighten up," is one of the comments he received on a recent 360-degree feedback report conducted as part of a leadership development program sponsored by his agency. "He is too serious and everyone feels uncomfortable around him. He should just smile or laugh once in a while."

The Best Medicine

When you were a kid and your parents were mad at each other or arguing, do you remember how it made you feel? They didn't need to say a word, but the heaviness and thickness of the energy was palpable. Their facial expressions added to the tone, but the somberness and emotion did not need to be voiced. It was felt. You reacted by laying low. You understood that asking for a ride or money or whether a friend could stay over wasn't a good idea.

Energy is tangible—we can feel it—and the tone of energy is contagious. Your energy as a leader is like a barometer for your team. If you are serious about treating Energy Breakdown in your organization, monitoring the quality and tone of your own energy is a critical component of the plan.

What mood do you convey each day?

Are you harried, gloomy, or intense? Is everything do-or-die and heavy? Or do you try to lighten the mood by not taking yourself and every situation too seriously?

Slowing down to smile and laugh and enjoy the moment breaks down negative energy and allows a positive charge to permeate the air. Before you know it, your mood changes and you set a new tone.

This part of the Energy Breakdown treatment plan is quite simple, and can be summed up with one simple question: as the leader, when you enter the room, others are watching and emulating—what type of energy and tone do you want to set?

Treatment Application:
Laugh: Questions to Ask Yourself

1. Do you smile at others to show your interest, warmth, and approachability?

2. Do you find humor in your human failings or mishaps, or are you usually mortified and embarrassed by them?

3. When something doesn't go as you planned, do you find yourself getting quite upset?

4. Do you believe that taking some time to talk to people about their lives or weekend plans is a waste of valuable time?

5. Are you constantly rushing from one thing to another, with a sense of anxiety as you try to keep up?

6. Do you try to lighten the mood in meetings that seem too formal and serious?

7. Do you try to have fun with others when working on things?

8. Is the tone you set playful at times, or is it all work and no play?

9. What types of things do you do on a daily basis to have fun?

10. Do you find something to smile or laugh about at least once a day?

Treatment Application:
Tips to Stop Taking Yourself So Seriously

1. When you approach someone, look at him or her in the eye and imagine a positive interaction.

2. When you make a mistake or do something that embarrasses you in front of others, remember that you are human. Everyone in the room is human and can relate.

3. Stop catastrophizing and imagining the worst.

4. Take a moment each day to look at something in nature like a beautiful sunset or a magnificent tree and wonder at their beauty.

5. Set an intention for the type of day you want to manifest each day. Make sure you monitor your behaviors to match the tone.

6. Stop ruining your day or getting riled up about things over which you have no control. If someone cuts you off in traffic, do you really want to carry that angry, resentful energy for the rest of the morning?

7. Remember that your behavior is always your choice. So is the attitude you bring with that behavior.

8. Think about whether your actions characterize a victim or a hero. Ask yourself which role you want to play as a leader in your organization and in your life.

9. Stop feeling sorry for yourself and start counting the things for which you are grateful.

10. Each day, identify one fun thing you can do at work and one fun thing you can do at home. Do them.

Ailment #5: Energy Breakdown

Leadership Remedy:
Balance—Honor Your Energy

Treatment Plan:

- Listen
- Limits
- Laugh

Prognosis:
Advice Following Treatment

Energy Breakdown Prognosis: *Advice Following Treatment*

Energy Breakdown is an ailment in organizations that affects every aspect of our lives. The consequence of ignoring our physical bodies and the quality and tone of the energy inside ourselves—our "energetic presence"—has rippling repercussions.

Making superhuman demands on our physical containers, otherwise known as the human body, has sustained negative impact over time.

As energetic beings, the quality of our energy has an enormous effect on our overall wellbeing, relationships, life and job satisfaction, and ultimate happiness.

Pushing ourselves when we're running on empty and negative is a sure way to propagate Energy Breakdown. We operate like empty batteries, fueled by nothing but caffeine and interacting in zombie-like, lifeless states.

If Robot Syndrome wasn't bad enough, Energy Breakdown constitutes an even worse manifestation of the loss of our human life force. The long-term effect is burnout. You can see it in the lack of life, passion, vitality, and excitement in organizations everywhere. People go through the motions yet are too burnt-out and run ragged to be charged up about anything. When combined with Robot Syndrome, the prognosis is dire.

The good news is that if Robot Syndrome is being treated and kept under control, the complementary treatments for Energy Breakdown can work wonders.

Practicing the three-fold treatment of . . .

- Listening to the signals your body sends you and taking care of yourself,

- Limiting how much you can take on at one time and setting realistic priorities, and

- Laughing more, lightening up, and monitoring the quality, tone, and charge of your own energy

. . . will enable you to model the way for your organization and encourage the same behaviors in others. The increase in vitality will ultimately have an amazing impact on the quality of your overall results and long-term engagement.

In Closing

My intent with this book is not to create a new leadership theory or wow you with new research. Nothing outlined in *The Cure* is new or complicated. In fact, the premise is quite simple.

My goal is to highlight for you what is really going on in your organization, to call it like it is and let you see yourself as the emperor or empress with no clothes. Can you picture yourself—a well-intentioned, talented, smart, and high-achieving but naked emperor? It's probably not too far from the truth.

By now, you should be able to spot and recognize the following five ailments quite easily:

1. The Robot Syndrome

2. "In No One We Trust" Toxicity

3. Yes-itis

4. Blame Disorder

5. Energy Breakdown

You should also be able to recognize the corresponding leadership behaviors that can be the antidote to these ailments if practiced and applied:

1. Connection

2. Authenticity

3. Empowerment

4. Accountability

5. Balance

My intent with *The Cure* is to ignite a fire in you. I want this book to be your wake up call, to show you how your leadership inertia and day-to-day behavioral choices affect the health of your organization with long-term and far-reaching effects on employee engagement, productivity, and overall results.

You already know what it takes to be a great leader. Now you know what I know—that inside each and every leader are the answers to the ailments rampant in their organizations.

As leader, you can choose to create an environment of connection, you can choose to be authentic, you can choose to empower those around you. As leader, you can hold yourself and others accountable and maintain the balance necessary for the long-term wellbeing of your organization.

As leader, you are *The Cure*.

About the Author

Janet Ioli is president of The Mana Group (TMG), LLC, a company providing leadership and organizational development services.

Janet is an executive coach, leadership and organizational development consultant, and an engaging speaker and workshop leader. Her experience helping people become better leaders and navigate through change spans more than 25 years. She has designed and led a myriad of executive leadership programs, provided one-on-one or group executive coaching, created strategies and processes to improve organizational effectiveness, and led human resources and leadership development and talent management functions in Fortune 200 companies.

With her extensive experience working with executives and as a senior human resources leader in three Fortune 200 companies in different industries, Janet has first-hand knowledge of the realities, situations, and complexities executives face leading organizations. She "gets it" and understands the context in which her clients operate. She has worked with and coached leaders in manufacturing, banking, military, insurance, government, publishing, media, government contracting, and information technology industries and has lived and worked in Greece and Germany.

In addition, Janet is an adjunct faculty member and executive coach at American University's School of Public Affairs. She teaches leadership courses and provides coaching in the Key Executive Leadership Program for government executives working in federal agencies. She is also on the adjunct faculty at the University of Maryland's Smith School of Business Advanced Executive Coaching program, designed for certified, experienced executive coaches nationwide.

Janet holds dual Master's degrees in Business and Public Administration and has completed coursework towards a PhD in Adult Learning & Human Development. She has earned a host of professional certifications and has participated in various certificate and training programs, including ones in coaching, organizational development, training design, facilitation, several 360 feedback instruments, emotional intelligence, FIRO-B, and the Myers-Briggs Type Indicator.

She is certified by the International Coaching Federation and has years of ongoing coach training, including an advanced executive coaching certificate for experienced, certified executive coaches at the University of Maryland's Smith School of Business. She has been using and providing feedback to leaders on assessment tools and 360 feedback instruments for more than 20 years and has deep practical and academic knowledge of leadership, group dynamics, and human psychology and development.

Janet's strength is giving leaders honest, relevant, and direct feedback, asking them the hard questions, and inspiring them to find their own answers. She provokes people to do the deep work needed to become more effective leaders in their organizations and, ultimately, their lives.

For more information, contact her at janet@themanagroup.com or visit her Web site at www.themanagroup.com.

Acknowledgements

My Muses

In Greek mythology, the muses were daughters of Zeus, the king of all the gods, and the goddesses of inspiration. They breathed the life of inspiration into mortal minds to enable and provoke the creation of art, poetry, writing, science, and all other such works for human understanding and enjoyment. Inspiration's source was not a mortal one—it was birthed in the realm of the heavens and sent down through the goddesses into human vessels to translate its meaning and essence into vehicles of enjoyment.

These heavenly catalysts, or muses, are sent to us in the most unlikely forms. My personal modern day muses have inspired me by providing me with life lessons, and have taken the following shapes:

Gabriella

My dear friend Emily's daughter, who died tragically on the playground of her elementary school in 2009 at the age of 10, haunts me with the stark reminder of the fragility and temporary nature of our human lives. The ghost of her un-lived life cut so short prods me to remind us all to live each moment with gusto and awe and create meaningful contributions while we can.

Family

Some of the biological and non-biological family relationships present in my life have taught me that people are individuals regardless of where they are born, who their parents are, and how they are socialized or raised. We each have the ability to choose our beliefs, actions, and paths in life, and the ones we learn early on need not define who we become. We all are responsible for looking at ourselves; no-one else can go on the uniquely individual journey of self-discovery, self-awareness, and self-development for us.

My work

Each day in my work life has been a living laboratory of research and lessons. The many leaders I have encountered over the past 25 or so years serve as models, examples, and teachers of the pains and realities present in our adult developmental journeys towards true self-authoring and leadership.

Books

Too many authors' words to mention have lit up my mind, heart, and soul since I was old enough to read. The wisdom I have gleaned over the years from these familiar souls has served as kindle wood, sparking countless connections and life applications, and lighting the flame of my own creativity within me.

Greece

I find it to be no accident that I was born in Athens, Greece. The first time I learned the teachings of the great philosophers of the ancient School of Athens, I was awestruck by the fact that I was in a place where I could actually walk in their footsteps and touch the same rocks of the buildings they traversed and conversed in. Socrates, Plato, and Aristotle served as my adolescent rock stars, their names and writings as familiar to me as the words to a popular billboard topping song.

My Musings of Gratitude

At the end of a book, one can usually find some sort of acknowledgment or expression of gratitude to the people who contributed to the author's ability to complete his/her authoring endeavor. My expressions of gratitude go out to:

- Maria Priles, my high school English Teacher at ACS who introduced me to the words of Emerson, Thoreau, Walt Whitman, Lord Byron, F. Scott Fitzgerald, and of course, Shakespeare's tragic hero leaders

- George Pisanias, my high school Greek teacher, who introduced me to Socrates and Plato and opened up a whole world of philosophy and ancient wisdom to me

- Dr. Marcie Boucouvalas, my PhD program professor at Virginia Tech who introduced me to the world of adult development, consciousness studies, and transpersonal psychology

- Edie Seashore, the organization development guru who taught me much about organizations, change, and the use of yourself as an instrument when helping organizations and people with change

- My colleagues and friends, Lara Zauner, Gretchen Cioffi, Laura Cassidy, Robin Baker, Kim Jojokian, Lonney Gregory, and so many others who provided encouraging words and votes of confidence during the years of my book writing endeavor

- Matt McGovern, editor extra-ordinaire, whose edits made my work sing louder than I ever could

- . . . and to Frank, whose support, love, and encouragement make me grateful every day.